IS IT

SUPPOSED

TO BE THIS

HARD?

Telling the Difference Between Emotional Abuse
and the Hard Work of Relationship

Mary Pat Haffey, MS

MAEVE BOOKS
emotionalabusebook.com
Atlanta, GA

Copyright © 2022 by Mary Pat Haffey

ISBN 979-8-9866369-0-0

This publication is meant as a source of valuable information for the reader, however it is not meant as a substitute for direct expert assistance. If such level of assistance is required, the services of a competent professional should be sought.

Edited by Sage Taylor Kingsley

Cover design by Flybolt

Interior formatting by KUHN Design Group

To my father, Peter John Valaer,
whose tender love was my saving grace.

CONTENTS

PREFACE

In preparation for writing this book, I put out a call through professional listservs for volunteers to share their stories about emotional abuse in the context of intimate partnerships. Since the facts and definition of emotional abuse are already well documented, the purpose of calling for volunteers was not to find subjects for a study, but rather to accrue a body of first-hand accounts to illustrate my points in a way that would speak directly to my readers.

I specifically asked for volunteers who had made some progress in healing from the abuse. In addition to sharing their experiences with emotional abuse, this group also provided insights into the healing and recovery process. As my work progressed and began to take a more defined shape, I put out another call, this time asking for people who not only had made progress toward recovery but who subsequently also had gotten into healthy relationships. Along with the experiences and insights offered by the first round of interviewees, this group was helpful in answering the question, "What is the difference between emotional abuse and the hard work of relationship?"

Of the twenty-eight people who contributed to this book:

- Nineteen went on to form relationships they identified as healthy.

- Twenty-six had gotten therapy, joined support groups, and/or read self-help books on emotional abuse. The other two found help through philosophical reading and a spiritual community. The wisdom they all gained from the various helpers and resources they encountered is evident in the insights they share.

- Twenty people experienced abuse in their families of origin. Five denied family of origin abuse but described feeling diminished in the general family dynamic. Two said they had a good family life growing up. One was not sure.

- Eight of the abused partners were the primary wage earners in the family.

- For nine people, the emotional abuse eventually became physical.

- The age at the time the abusive relationship began ranged from fourteen to fifty-eight: four were still in their teens, ten in their twenties, ten in their thirties, three in their forties, and one was fifty-eight. Four had more than one abusive partnership before they got the help they needed to learn healthier ways to be in relationship.

Without my purposely seeking diversity in gender orientations, the twenty-eight people interviewed included two lesbians, two gay men, one bisexual, one person who identified as queer who was abused by a transgender male partner, and three heterosexual men abused by female partners. It is my hope that emotionally abused people of all gender identities will be able to relate to the experiences described in this book. Consequently, I am forgoing the grammatically correct his/her/he/she pronoun constructions in favor of the gender non-specific "they." As much as possible, I use plural nouns to agree with the plural pronoun, but there are instances where that is not feasible.

In another deviation from standard practices, I have put citation material in endnotes rather than the traditional parentheses within the body of the text in order to make the book more readable.

Because spoken language is sometimes repetitive and tangential, I have edited some quotes for clarity, but in each case I have strived to stay true to the speaker's original message. A few quotes are composites of similar statements. Composite quotes have been assigned the initials: "CQ."

All volunteers signed informed consent forms. All names have been changed, and personal details have been omitted or changed to protect privacy. In many cases I did not know the name of the interviewee's abusive partner. For the sake of clarity, there are some anecdotes in which I assign a name to the abuser as well as the abused partner; all such names are purely fictitious.

ACKNOWLEDGMENTS

First, I would like to thank the twenty-eight people who generously gave their time and courageously told their stories. They provided a rich and deep pool of experiences for me to draw on, and this book would not have been possible without them. One of the hard parts of my work was the necessity of leaving out so much of their stories as I shaped the narrative for this book.

I also want to express my appreciation for the few people who initially volunteered, and then decided that telling their stories was more than they could do at the time. Recognizing and stating boundaries is an important part of healing from abuse and deserves to be honored.

I am grateful to the many beta readers who shared their insightful comments and constructive criticisms, including: Venecia Heron, Maggie Joffe, Shelley Jordan, Kristyn McGeehan, and Tasha Messer. There are others who were abused partners and whose names shall remain anonymous; you know who you are. Many thanks to all of you.

In addition, I wish to thank my colleagues, Denise Houston, LPC; Margaret Moore, Ed D; and Linda Weiskoff, LCSW, who were also beta readers. They were all generous with their time, feedback, and encouragement. A special thanks to Linda, who has been an ongoing source of support from the earliest stages of this project.

Thanks also go to my writers' group, especially the leader, Anne Bartolucci, PhD, who provided valuable information and guidance on the process of self-publishing.

Finally, I want to thank my family and friends who patiently and empathically listened as I discussed my plans, progress, fears, and frustrations in many, many conversations. In particular, I wish to acknowledge my son, Joel Haffey, who was always available to help with technical support when I needed it, and my sister, Kate Valaer, who proofread large portions of the work.

I have no doubt that this book is better because of the contributions of each of these caring people.

INTRODUCTION

I knew that the things he was doing were hurtful, and I knew I didn't like them, and I wished he wouldn't do them, but I would not have used the word abusive.

— SAMANTHA

I tried different things, lots of trial and error, and failed attempts in spite of my best efforts. It wasn't until after leaving the situation that I would have used the word abuse.

— ABIGAIL

Like Samantha and Abigail, most emotionally abused partners don't know they are being abused.

What they do know is that they've been trying everything they can think of to make their relationship better.

They know too that they experience a great deal of frustration as their efforts consistently fail to create the closeness and mutual understanding they strive for.

They know they are often confused by their partner's behavior and what is going on in the relationship.

They know they repeatedly feel hurt without fully understanding why.

They know they feel baffled or stunned when their partner, once

13

again, openly says or does something hurtful with seemingly little or no provocation.

They know they feel hopeful and reassured when their partner intermittently shows a loving, caring side, or things simply seem to be back on an even keel.

They know they frequently have a walking-on-eggshells feeling because they are never quite sure when or why the switch from loving to hurtful will happen.

They know they often feel lonely even though they are in an intimate relationship.

And because of all of the above, they regularly wonder what is wrong with them.

If you recognize yourself in the above description, this is the book for you.

Most emotionally abused people think they are just dealing with the kinds of relationship issues all couples face. They usually feel shock, disbelief, and shame when they realize the relationship difficulties they have struggled with are actually due to the fact that their trusted life partner is emotionally abusive. They wonder how it is possible they didn't know this—and why they tolerated the mistreatment as long as they did.

I have three goals in mind with this book. One is to help people tell the difference between emotional abuse and the hard work of relationship; the next is to validate the abused partner's experience and minimize or eliminate the shame and judgment they often feel by explaining why emotional abuse is so hard to recognize; and the third is to help people discover ways to claim, or reclaim, a sense of strength and empowerment that was so badly eroded by the abuse.

Chapter 1, "Definition: *I Didn't Think of It as Abuse,*" takes a detailed look at what emotional abuse is. By combining the work of widely recognized experts in the field and the voices of emotionally abused partners, I discuss the definition of emotional abuse and how it manifests in the lives of those who have experienced it. Building upon the work of John Gottman, a specialist in marriage therapy, I contrast a list of abusive tactics with how healthy couples treat each other. Finally, I explain why the Cycle of Violence Wheel is not a reliable indicator of emotional abuse.

Chapter 2, "The Unspoken Contract and Common Wisdom: *'I'm Doing What I'm Supposed to Do. Why Isn't It Working?,'*" examines how common wisdom about relationships plays a part in forming an unspoken, unconscious, and unequal relationship contract that works against abused partners and makes it difficult to recognize the abuse. It explains how the very behaviors that support a healthy relationship are harmful to the partner in an abusive one.

Chapter 3, "Trust and the Ever-Changing Contract: *'Why Is This So Hard?,'*" explores the fundamental human need for trust in intimate relationships and how abusers violate that trust. It also describes how the abuser's unpredictable shifts from loving to abusive behaviors are part of the abuse process and can lead to traumatic bonding.

Chapter 4, "Unspoken Contracts and the Family of Origin: *'I Thought It Was Just Part of Being Married,'*" looks at what children from abusive families learn about relationships. It addresses how those experiences affect both abusive and abused partners and how they influence the interactions between couples in abusive partnerships.

Subtlety is such a pervasive aspect of emotional abuse that it takes two chapters to discuss it. Chapter 5, "Subtlety Part I: *'But It's Not That Bad,'*" shows how emotional abuse blends with everyday interactions in such a way that abused partners are not even sure it is happening. Chapter 6, "Subtlety Part II: *'But Others Have It So Much Worse,'*" discusses how more egregious abuses such as abusive anger, financial abuse, isolation, abandonment, and sexual abuse can be practiced in subtle ways, leaving the abused partner unsure if they are really abusive. Both chapters help people discern subtle emotional abuse and explain why emotionally abused partners often don't know they are being abused.

Chapter 7, "Denial: *Am I Going Crazy?*,'" validates abused people by showing how denial obscures the reality of the abuse. It explores how gaslighting and passive-aggressive behaviors undermine and confuse abused partners, depleting their confidence in their own perceptions, good judgment, and self-concept. It also addresses the partner's denial.

Chapter 8, "Telling the Difference: *Could This Be Emotional Abuse?*,'" reviews many abusive behaviors described in previous chapters and contrasts them with the ways in which people in healthy relationships treat each other. It provides clear markers to help people distinguish between emotional abuse and the hard work of relationship.

Chapter 9, "Normalizing: *How Could I Have Let This Happen?*,'" takes an in-depth look at how judgment from self and others adds to the impact of emotional abuse. It discusses how family of origin dynamics can predispose people to accept abuse, dispels myths about what causes abuse, and validates abused partners by pointing out that people in abusive relationships share similar experiences and react in similar ways.

Chapter 10, "The Path to Empowerment: *I Am Honoring Me Today*,'" outlines various steps people can take to reclaim their power—whether they leave the relationship or feel the need to stay. It includes sections on acknowledging the abuse, detaching from the abuser, setting boundaries, and taking action steps toward greater self-reliance and self-respect.

"A Note to Heterosexual Men" uses firsthand accounts to describe ways in which emotionally abusive heterosexual women use traditional male roles and stereotypes to abuse their male partners.

There are Activity questions throughout the book. Answering those questions can help you discern if your relationship is abusive and strengthen your resolve and conviction as you move toward greater empowerment. Chapter 10 asks you to refer to the answers to these questions as part of the recovery process.

It can also be helpful to journal or just make brief notes about memories and reactions that come up for you while you are reading. If you feel a paper journal may be invaded by an abusive partner, consider keeping a digital journal behind a password via your phone, email, or some other way.

This book may be difficult to read for anyone still living with emotional abuse. For those who have left an abusive relationship, it may trigger acute reactions. It is important to honor your process and take as many breaks as necessary to keep your equilibrium. Reading the book in conjunction with therapy or support meetings can be helpful.

You don't need to read the chapters in order. You may choose to look at the Table of Contents and begin by reading the sections that seem most relevant to you. Or you may look at the summaries here to guide you as to where to jump in. You may also skim through and focus on the quotes from other abused partners. All the people whose stories are in here have taken steps toward healing, and many have gone on to form healthy relationships. You may find encouragement in what they share.

It is my hope that this book will help you tell the difference between emotional abuse and the hard work of relationship, understand yourself more, judge yourself less, increase your confidence in deciding whether to go or stay, empower yourself, and be better able to recognize signs of an abuser in a new relationship. You deserve kindness and respect. Always. Let's begin.

CHAPTER 1

DEFINITION

"I Didn't Think of It as Abuse"

I didn't view it as abusive as much as hurtful. I know it is the same thing, but I was viewing it as, "That is an awful hurtful thing to say. If he cares about me, why is he saying these things to me? Why is he accusing me of something I didn't do?" If I brought it up in front of other people, he would say, "You know I would never be that way." So, it was very confusing, too. But I didn't view it as abusive until it started to get physical, and then I started thinking, "This is abuse."

—WARREN

L ike Warren, you may often feel hurt by your partner but don't think it amounts to something that could be called abusive. And there is a good chance that your partner, although hurtful at times, is not *all* bad. In fact, there may still be things you really enjoy and value in the relationship, and better times you hope to get back. Finally, you may believe that if you can only figure out what keeps going wrong, you and your partner will be able to work things out, and the relationship will be closer to what you hoped it would be.

There are many good reasons for your confusion. Emotional abuse is subtle and easily denied. In addition, it is often mistaken for the misunderstandings and common conflicts most couples have. After all, we are told that relationships are hard work, and that healthy couples stick together in good times and bad.

Therefore, it's important to discern: "What is emotional abuse, and how is it different from the hard work of relationship?"

Beverly Engel (1990), a specialist in the field of emotional abuse, provides a definition that helps answer that question. She tells us that:

> "True emotional abuse is distinguished by the following:
>
> It is constant, as opposed to occasional.
>
> The intent is to devalue and denigrate rather than to simply state a complaint.
>
> The intent is to dominate and control rather than to provide constructive criticism.
>
> The person has an overall attitude of disrespect toward you, rather than just not liking something specific that you are doing." (p. 22)

WHETHER AN IMPULSE OR A PLAN, IT IS STILL ABUSE

Interestingly, it is not only abused partners who don't recognize emotional abuse for what it is. Engel (2002) adds to the definition, saying emotional abuse is "any behavior or attitude that emotionally damages another person, regardless of whether there is conscious intent to do so" (p. 41). Lundy Bancroft (2002), a therapist who specializes in working with abusive men, agrees that abuse is abuse whether it is conscious or not; however, he holds that while the motivation for abuse may be unconscious, the behavior is intentional.

In practice it can be a combination of both. In the following example with Terri and John, it is likely that neither one recognized the first part of the encounter as abusive, but the statement at the end was clearly designed to hurt:

We were on a car trip with our infant son, driving along the highway at about 60 miles per hour. Just as we were approaching a military base on the other side of a large stand of trees, the baby started fussing and wanted to nurse. (This was before the time when we knew the importance of car seats for babies.) John adamantly insisted that I wait because one of the soldiers at the base might see me nursing. Given the speed of the car and the distance from the base with the obstruction of the trees, I knew he was being irrational. When I pointed out that what he was worried about couldn't possibly happen, he got more agitated. Honestly, at this point I can't really remember if I was intimidated by his intensity or humoring him, or a little of both, but I comforted the baby the best I could for several minutes. Then, instead of saying, "It's ok now," or something like that, he kind of sneered and said, "Why don't you stick a boob in that kid's mouth?" I was stunned and stung. It felt like he hit me for no reason. I was, after all, waiting to feed the baby because of him.

The attitude of abuse is seen in John's disregard for his wife and child. He was willing to put them in distress for the sake of his own comfort. Maybe he didn't realize he was engaging in a controlling act. But notice, he did not politely ask his wife to wait before nursing the baby. He did not say he would feel better if she waited, and his tone created an undercurrent of intimidation for her. Perhaps he was so wrapped up in his own point of view that he didn't think what he was doing was abusive. But his words, "Why don't you stick a boob in that kid's mouth?" show a clear *intention* to demean his partner. And Terri, while willing to accommodate her husband to calm his growing agitation, clearly saw his final comment as a problem.

This leads us to a major point of confusion in discerning emotional abuse from the hard work of relationship: Don't all relationships have their problems? Aren't they something that people just need to work through?

How can we tell the difference?

IT HAPPENS REPEATEDLY

It is true that people sometimes lash out unfairly at their mates when stress, frustration, or exhaustion push them beyond their limits. And it is the rare couple that never gets into a heated argument, ultimately saying or doing things that are hurtful and that they later regret. It is also true that some couples fight more than others, so it can be hard to discern if you are in an abusive relationship or just one that is more emotionally reactive than others.

It is the *repetitive* pattern of the abusive events that distinguishes emotional abuse from the sometimes hurtful things that happen in most relationships. Words like ongoing, consistent, systematic, habitual, and pattern are regularly used to describe emotional abuse, while words like occasional and isolated event are reserved for the inevitable hurts that happen every so often between healthier couples.[1]

IT'S ABOUT POWER AND CONTROL

In addition to the habitual nature of emotional abuse, experts agree that the impulse for power and control is what motivates abusers to denigrate their partners.[2]

Whether they are driven by extreme insecurity, anxiety, systemic misogyny, family of origin experiences, addictions, narcissism, or other psychological conditions, their coping mechanisms are the same: dominating and demeaning their partners to meet their own psychological needs. In the process, they show little or no concern for the pain their quest for control has on the other person.

People who are abusive construct this power-over position by using methods that go far beyond the typical transgressions and missteps that occur in mutually respectful relationships.

IT CAN BE BOTH
UNDERCOVER AND OPEN

The above example with Terri and John reveals both the blatant and subtle aspects of emotional abuse. As abusers seek dominance over their partners, they draw upon a vast array of tactics ranging from the very subtle, like using an increasingly agitated mood to coerce compliance with their wishes, to making blatantly hurtful statements, and on to raging and threatening to do harm.

In some cases, abusers engage in an orchestrated set of behaviors that amount to brainwashing, sometimes even gaining enough influence to force their partners to participate in illegal activities.[3]

Subtle abuse tactics are insidious and make up the background atmosphere in an emotionally abusive household. They create a slow but constant drain on the partner's emotional and mental resources, leaving them less able to cope with more openly aggressive assaults when they come. The more obvious events are often mistaken for the kinds of misunderstandings, communication problems, or squabbles that most couples deal with from time to time.

But in an emotionally abusive relationship these are often purposeful, if sometimes unconscious, attempts to undermine the partner in order to affirm a sense of power and control for the abuser.

COMPARING ABUSIVE AND
HEALTHY RELATIONSHIPS

In trying to distinguish between the "hard work of relationship" and emotional abuse, it can be helpful to see how healthy couples treat each other compared to how abusers treat their partners. John Gottman, a renowned researcher and marriage therapist, has documented specific ways in which happy couples in stable relationships show love and respect for each other. The behaviors he describes stand in stark contrast to the way emotional abusers treat their partners. Put a check in each box that applies to your situation.

Abusers Show Disdain Instead of Affection

Gottman (1994), has observed that "affection exchanged through gestures, eye contact, and facial expressions" mark healthy relationships (p. 62).

Abusers, on the other hand, utilize non-verbal behaviors that show disdain rather than affection. Abusers will use:

☐ Disapproving looks—frowning, scowling, or rolling eyes

☐ Condescending or patronizing looks—for instance, showing a superior or parental attitude toward their partner

☐ Heavy sighs, showing impatience or exasperation

☐ Ignoring their partner's words, feelings, or even their very presence

☐ The silent treatment—refusing to engage for hours, days, or longer

Abusers Express Disregard Instead of Empathy

Gottman goes on to say that couples in happy relationships "express lots of empathy and sympathy for one another."

Abusers, instead, show disregard for their partners by:

☐ Belittling their interests, projects, friends, dreams, activities, goals, values, personality traits, or physical characteristics

☐ Denying their feelings—refusing to acknowledge their feelings, or claiming they aren't justified

☐ Using disparaging tones of voice

☐ Showing a lack of concern when the partner is ill or injured, sad, or stressed

☐ Rejecting overtures for connection through conversation, time together, or intimacy

☐ Dismissing and devaluing their contributions to the household, or their personal and professional achievements

Abusers Devalue Instead of Value Their Partners

Gottman also notes that people in strong relationships are appreciative of each other, even brag about the other's skills and accomplishments (pp. 60-62).

Rather than showing appreciation for their partners, abusers undermine their self-worth by devaluing and diminishing them. For example:

☐ Minimizing, flatly denying, or ignoring positive attributes

☐ Emphasizing or exaggerating flaws, or even assigning faults and negative traits that aren't true of their partner

☐ Saying false things to others about their partner in order to paint them in a negative light

☐ Regularly criticizing and judging; this can be done covertly under the guise of being concerned or helpful

☐ Making insulting comments and put-downs: stupid, fat, ugly, clumsy, incompetent, no one would want you

☐ Shaming, guilt-tripping

☐ Refusing to give credit where credit is due

☐ Ridiculing

☐ Humiliating in private or public

☐ Not seeing their partner as an individual—treating them as an extension of the abuser, or as a stereotype

☐ Showing disinterest in what the other has to say

Abusers Derail Conflicts Instead of Resolving Them

Another quality Gottman identifies in healthy couples is the "ability to resolve the conflicts that are inevitable in any relationship." He adds, "I believe we grow in our relationships by reconciling our differences" (p. 28).

But emotional abusers are not interested in communication and problem solving because their drive for power and control is the very source of the problem, and they don't want to acknowledge what they are doing or stop doing it. Instead, they refuse to honestly address the issues by:

☐ Denying anything is wrong

☐ Accusing and blaming—to redirect attention away from their abusive behavior and onto the partner

☐ Refusing to negotiate or compromise—like walking away or unilaterally declaring the conversation is over

☐ Simply refusing to acknowledge their partner's part of a conversation

☐ Using anger to create a dramatic uproar that justifies walking away

☐ Arguing to intimidate and silence the other rather than communicate and persuade

☐ Derailing the discussion by arguing irrelevant points and changing the subject

☐ Purposely misinterpreting or twisting what was said for the sake of ending the discussion or getting it off track and changing the topic

Abusers Engage In Power Plays Instead of Showing Consideration

Gottman (2018) talks about consideration between loving couples, saying, "We aren't negotiating for the best deal just for ourselves. We're always considering the cost of any choice for our partner, too" (p. 51).

Far from being considerate of their partners, abusers engage in a wide variety of power plays at the expense of their partner's emotional wellness. For instance:

☐ Manipulating—using undercover means to influence someone's behavior for self-serving purposes without the other's knowledge

☐ Gaslighting—a particular kind of manipulation in which the abuser covertly attempts to make their partner feel crazy or unsure of themselves, their ideas, thoughts, perceptions, and/or judgments

☐ Using double binds—setting up a situation so their partner is wrong no matter what they do, also known as a Catch-22

☐ Acting on a sense of privilege or entitlement—for instance, refusing to share fairly in household chores, giving orders, making important decisions without consulting their partner, using double standards ("I can lose my temper, you can't.")

☐ Ignoring agreements—changing plans with little or no notice, not following through on promises or agreements, even denying there was such an agreement, or twisting it

☐ Withholding information—for the sake of deceiving, blind-siding, controlling, or just to derive a sense of power from knowing something the other doesn't

☐ Sabotaging intimate moments—for instance, disparaging a body trait right after sex, comparing sexual performance or body shape to someone else, or rejecting sexual over-tures in a harsh or demeaning manner

☐ Exploiting vulnerabilities—threatening to leave someone who has long-standing fears of abandonment or making alarming statements to someone who has anxiety issues

☐ Pressuring their partner to participate in activities they have clearly stated they do not want to do

☐ Isolating their partner from family and friends, or from work/school opportunities

Abusers Create Uncertainty and Risk Instead of Trust and Safety

Finally, Gottman points out, "Couples whose relationships are successful feel safe with each other" (p. 216).

Below are examples of how abusers undermine a sense of emotional, financial, or physical safety in a relationship:

☐ Showing signs of building anger—clenched teeth or fists, for example (The increasing agitation John displayed about his wife nursing exemplifies this tactic.)

☐ Expressing anger or aggression with little or no provocation

☐ Raging—out of control fury, rapidly approaching or towering over the other while in a fit of anger. Yelling in another's face

☐ Poking at the other's chest while yelling at them. Shaking a finger or fist in the other's face

☐ Punching holes in doors or walls, throwing, damaging, or breaking furniture or other household items

☐ Relentlessly following and yelling at someone who wants a timeout from the discord

☐ Doing things to retaliate when their partner doesn't comply with their wishes, such as destroying, hiding, or damaging things they value

☐ Interfering with the ability to sleep

☐ Badgering

☐ Name-calling

☐ Unrelentingly criticizing their partner

☐ Incurring debt without the other's knowledge

☐ Depriving their partner of resources—limiting access to money, taking the car keys away, changing the house lock, or disabling the car, computer, phone, or other necessary device

☐ Acting overly jealous or possessive—stalking; checking their partner's phone, emails, journals; constantly calling to check their whereabouts; demanding that they account for their time away; accusing them of infidelity with no objective evidence

☐ Driving unsafely to frighten or intimidate

☐ Threatening physical abuse to their partner, or the partner's children, friends, family, or pets

☐ Displaying or referencing a weapon during an argument, or to otherwise intimidate

MORE ABOUT HOW IT HAPPENS

As daunting as that list may seem, it is not comprehensive. Abusers can get very creative about finding ways to dominate their partner.

Subtle tactics are veiled in everyday interactions like underhanded jokes or sowing self-doubt with statements such as, "I don't know what you see in him/her/that …" or, "You want to join the choir? You do know you have to audition for that, right? I'd hate for you to embarrass yourself." Or, "You've never been very good at that. Let me do it for you."

A steady diet of undermining comments from a trusted loved one begins to erode a person's self-confidence without their ever noticing it is happening. Even if the partner can see an abusive tactic for what it is and discover a way to sidestep or stop it, abusers will devise yet another way to achieve power over their partners.

Frequently, several abusive techniques are blended together in a single incident. For example, the abuser in the following anecdote landed several emotional blows at the same time, some open, others more subtle.

> We needed a new refrigerator. This was back in the day when
> there were three colors to choose from: avocado green, copper,
> and gold. We were standing in the appliance department with
> the salesperson, and I said I was trying to figure out which
> color would be more versatile in case I wanted to redecorate
> the kitchen some time. My husband scowled at me and said,

"I'm not buying you a new refrigerator every time you want to paint the walls," then turned around and walked off. Even the salesman said, "That's not what she said."

— TERRI

The open methods of abuse this person used include:

Blindsiding—the partner was shocked by a verbal assault that seemed to come out of nowhere.

Public humiliation—The husband belittled his wife in front of the salesman, who felt the need to come to her rescue: "That's not what she said."

Controlling assets—"I'm not going to buy you...." The abuser claimed the right to unilaterally bestow or withhold necessary household resources.

Twisting what the partner said in order to argue against a nonexistent point.

And covertly the abuser was:

Criticizing his wife for a trait that was not true of her. Prudence (carefully choosing a versatile color) was treated like a frivolous impulse.

Shaming—the husband sends the message, "You want unreasonable things. You are a demanding and irrational person."

Treating a household appliance like a personal indulgence, reducing the partner to a stereotype associated with the kitchen.

Ultimately, the abuser unilaterally ends the discussion by walking away.

By walking off, he shut down any possibility for a discussion, rejected his wife, and left her to make a major purchase alone while feeling the aftermath of his emotional assault.

SOMETIMES IT'S GRADUAL, SOMETIMES SUDDEN

Emotional abusers usually begin the abusive process gradually. It steadily grows in frequency and intensity, as they slowly undermine their partner's sense of self, reduce their defenses, and make them increasingly vulnerable to more openly aggressive verbal attacks. Since part of the definition of emotional abuse is that it is an ongoing process, it takes time and repeated offenses for that pattern to emerge.

Some of the more obvious abuses initially seem to be isolated events and are explained away (by both the abuser and abused) with excuses such as the abuser was overly stressed or tired and didn't mean what they said or did. By the time the abuse has gone on long enough to meet the definition of being a systemic part of the relationship, it has already begun to take a toll on the partner's sense of self.

Sometimes abusers apologize and promise that it won't happen again, although many never do. They do, however, have an uncanny ability to sense when they've gone a step too far and need to adjust their behavior to bring their partner back under their influence. That in itself becomes part of the disorienting abusive process: inspiring hope that things will go back to the way they were in happier times, while the undercover abuses are still occurring in the background, and the blatant abuses will appear again, sooner or later.

The onset of emotional abuse is not always gradual, however. Sometimes the abuse will suddenly ramp up when there is some kind of commitment that makes it more difficult for the abused partner to just walk away, like investing in a house together, getting married, having a baby, or moving to a new location where the abused partner is separated from their support system. Giving up a job to make such a move or to stay home with the children makes partners more dependent and opens another way for abusers to exert control over them.

IT CAN HAPPEN TO ANYONE

Sometimes abusers exploit other vulnerabilities, such as a difference in age, with the younger person being more inclined to believe what the abuser says. Or the abused partner may have a less prestigious education, a lower-paying job, or come from a less-elevated social situation. People who come into the relationship with low self-esteem, or who have vulnerabilities due to early childhood experiences or other traumas, are especially susceptible to manipulation by an abuser.

However, even people who are sure of themselves when they enter an abusive relationship can fall prey to the undermining and devaluing tactics of abuse, crumbling the confidence and self-esteem they had before, as Leticia explains:

> *Prior to my marriage, I was fun. I was carefree. I had so many friends. I was so active. We'd dance and go camping, relax, have fun. There were lots of friends and lots of laughter. And I noticed myself shutting down. I remember saying to my friends, "I used to be so fun." And I just lost all of that.*

Even people who have high-powered jobs and are strong and independent in the outside world can be on the receiving end of emotional abuse at home with the same devastating effects.

Denise tells about her status before the abuse started:

> *I had a booming career before my marriage. I was one of the first females to be doing my job running a department for a national chain.*

Once she gave up her job and moved to another state to start a life with her new husband, the denigration, disregard, and hurtful behaviors began and gradually increased over time. Another abused partner, Anika, reported being the primary wage earner in her family. She had a vibrant career in a highly respected position with an international company while she was experiencing abuse at home.

Both women described feeling profoundly diminished by the abuse. Regardless of the circumstances at the beginning of the relationship, abuse wears away at a person's self-worth and confidence in their perceptions, in the validity of their reactions, and in their own good judgment, ultimately hindering their ability to recognize the abuse for what it is.

VARIOUS STYLES OF ABUSE

Emotional abuse can show up in many ways. Some abusers will use most of the tactics described above frequently. Others will only use a few, and less often. Abusers who are addicts might only abuse when they are actively using. One partner explained that her husband's abuse mostly consisted of him ignoring her and refusing to talk about it, yet it affected her so profoundly she considered suicide. Some abusers rely primarily on anger and raging to intimidate their partners. Others are masters at manipulation and rarely raise their voices at all.

The relationship may be mostly abusive, or there may be good times between blatantly abusive events. Some abusers will become more caring when their partner is ill or down in the dumps; others will exploit any weakness for their own benefit. In addition, many abusers will change tactics randomly, making it difficult to anticipate or predict what will happen next.

A lot of abusive behavior is due to narcissism (for more on narcissism in domestic abuse see Morningstar on page 298). Although not all abusers are narcissists, there are certain narcissistic traits that are typical of abusers. Three that will be discussed at length in this book include the following:

- A sense of superiority and entitlement that results in a pattern of self-serving, controlling, and power-over behaviors

- A lack of empathy and compassion that manifests in a regularly recurring disregard and diminishment of their partners

- A failure to take responsibility for their behavior that leads to blaming, deflecting, denying, gaslighting, and other forms of manipulation

In addition, there are other psychological conditions that can lead to emotional abuse. For instance, Lachkar (see page 296) discusses how various personality disorders manifest in abusive behaviors, and Mason (see page 298) offers guidance to people who love someone with borderline personality disorder.

But it doesn't take a diagnosable disorder for abuse to happen. For example, an insecure person with high anxiety, low frustration tolerance, and poor anger management skills can be plenty abusive.

Regardless of an abuser's motivation, style, or tactics, the abuse is highly destructive to a partner's emotional, mental, and physical well-being.

SUMMARY

- In a healthy relationship, there is an overarching pattern of love, support, and respect with occasional hurtful instances.

- In an abusive relationship, there is an overarching pattern of disrespectful, controlling, and demeaning behaviors intermixed with times of love and kindness.

- It is the frequency of the hurtful events that can help someone affected by abuse to distinguish between the hard work of relationship and emotional abuse.

ACTIVITY

1. Look at the list of abusive behaviors and check any that you have experienced. Many emotional abusers mix good times in with the abuse, especially in the beginning, so don't discount the hurtful times because there are (or were) also some good times.

2. Do you regularly feel hurt, confused, shocked, or intimidated by these events?

3. How often do they happen? In a healthy relationship, hurtful events will be a rare occurrence. If they happen repeatedly, regularly, or often, you are likely experiencing emotional abuse.

4. To get a clearer picture of the ongoing pattern of emotional abuse, keep a calendar for one month, making a mark each time something hurtful happens, even if you are not sure why it was hurtful or whether it constitutes abuse.

It is not necessary to have experienced all or even most of these abusive tactics to be abused. Even a few experienced regularly will wear away at your level of confidence and diminish your self-worth, making you more vulnerable to further abuses over time.

IS IT SUPPOSED TO BE THIS HARD?

No. It shouldn't be an ongoing struggle to be respected as an equal partner, to be noticed and acknowledged, and to be treated with consideration on a regular basis. Sabrina, an abused partner who later got into a healthy relationship, shares her experience:

> *Relationships take hard work, but they don't take that kind of hard of work. When two people are invested in each other's happiness, and invested in moving forward, when they love each other, it's—yeah you have to do a lot of talking, but you talk, you open up and things move forward. I'm even talking about living with someone who is an alcoholic. My relationship is a million times easier than it was with the abuser, because we have good communication. He admits his shortcomings, and so do I. An abusive relationship takes so much work and yet nothing moves forward.*

NOTE: THE CYCLE OF VIOLENCE
AND EMOTIONAL ABUSE

One popular tool for explaining what happens in abusive relationships is the Cycle of Violence Wheel based on the work of Lenore Walker (1979). It includes a tension-building phase that leads to an openly abusive event, which is followed by remorse and reconciliation, and then a honeymoon phase. Eventually the tension starts to build again and the cycle repeats. However, emotionally abused partners who rely on this tool can be misled into thinking that they are not abused because it doesn't fit the pattern found in emotionally abusive relationships very well.

The pattern in emotional abuse is simply its repetitive nature. In what seems to be a contradiction, it is both repetitive and unpredictable. So, it happens again and again, but randomly. In fact, unpredictability is a characteristic of emotional abuse. For instance, in emotional abuse there is not necessarily a tension-building phase. Openly abusive events often happen with no warning whatsoever:

> *It's like living with a sniper. You never know what action you're going to take that is going to get you slaughtered.*
>
> —PAOLA

And they can also come and go quickly with a sharp retort or demeaning comment, then back to normal as if nothing happened. There is often no acknowledgment of the abuse, let alone contrition or reconciliation:

> *It's like a drive-by shooting. It happens. Then when it's over, they act like it never happened.*
>
> — TERRI

In addition, the manipulation, withdrawal, and passive-aggression that many emotional abusers use do not include physical violence or threats of violence, and they are ongoing rather than cyclical. What's more, with emotional abuse there are usually low-level abuses that happen consistently, even casually, without any tension-building involved. All those techniques leave an emotionally abused partner *feeling* abused without realizing that they are *being* abused:

He never raised his voice. It was all very subtle psychological abuse.

— JAYLA

It can be confusing because there are things that happen in emotional abuse that mimic the events in the Cycle of Violence Wheel. For instance, emotional abuse is usually intermingled with more pleasant, even loving, times that could be mistaken for the honeymoon phase. But those times are not necessarily related to a big abusive event followed by contrition and reconciliation as is more common with physical abuse.

Abusers who use anger as a control tactic often will show growing irritation to get their partners to comply with their wishes. Although that is tension building, it is different from the cycle of abuse tension-building phase in that there is a manipulative quality about it. The abuser may blow up no matter what their partner does to calm things, or they may ease up once they get their way. And a blowup is not necessarily, or even likely, followed by remorse and a honeymoon phase.

The aspect of emotional abuse that most closely follows a cycle is when angry outbursts are followed by an apology and forgiveness. Especially early in the relationship, abusers sometimes will apologize for an openly abusive event. But since abusers rarely change their behavior, apologies and forgiveness are inevitably followed by another offense, another apology, and more forgiveness. Even though this process repeats, it does not always include all the phases described in the cycle of abuse diagram, nor does it account for the randomness of emotional abuse. The same emotional abuser may apologize one time, then totally ignore that a similar offense took place another time. For all these reasons, the Cycle of Violence Wheel is not a reliable tool in determining if emotional abuse is taking place.

The National Domestic Violence Hotline offers confidential support to people experiencing emotional abuse, as well as those facing physical abuse. See page 297 for more information.

CHAPTER 2

THE UNSPOKEN CONTRACT AND COMMON WISDOM

"I'm Doing What I'm Supposed to Do. Why Isn't It Working?"

When you are trying to work with an abuser, everything is hard, hard work and you're the only one who is truly doing the work. Everything you are saying seems to be falling on deaf ears. And you are working in opposite directions. You're trying to be heard and have open communication and move forward, and he is trying to justify himself and placate you or something. But relationships shouldn't be that hard. If a relationship is really hard to the point where it feels impossible, then something is wrong.

—SABRINA

If you are in an emotionally abusive relationship, Sabrina's frustration will sound familiar to you. Do you, like her, feel as if your efforts to improve your relationship are mostly one-sided? Are you frequently discouraged and frustrated when you try to communicate with your partner about the problems between you? Does it often seem like your partner is working against you rather than with you? There is a reason why emotionally abused people feel like they and their partners are "working in opposite directions." It's because they are.

THE UNSPOKEN CONTRACT

Most human relationships include unconscious and unspoken agreements. Unlike oral or written contracts, unspoken relationship contracts are made without either person being fully aware of what they are agreeing to. These contracts are influenced by four things:

1. Common wisdom about what constitutes a good relationship

2. The innate drive of humans to connect with a trusted other— to love and be loved

3. Family of origin dynamics

4. The daily interactions that shape a couple's everyday life together

People come together to form intimate partnerships believing they and their beloved share mutual understandings about what makes a healthy, loving relationship; they believe they have a shared relationship contract. However, most couples soon discover that they also have plenty of misunderstandings about what a partnership should be, and that is where the hard work of relationship begins. With healthy couples, the relationship contract is based on a mutual commitment to the well-being of each person and the relationship as a whole, so they have a basic foundation for working through their differences. *In abusive relationships, there is no such mutual agreement, although one partner believes that there is.*

While abused partners trust that the person they love is working with them toward mutual well-being and a healthy relationship, abusers are taking advantage of that trust to gain a position of power over them. *This unspoken and unrecognized misalignment in the relationship contract sets up the essential, yet hidden power imbalance upon which the emotionally abusive relationship is based.* It allows abusers to subtly maneuver for dominance and control while their partners believe they are both involved in the work of building a loving, mutually supportive and respectful relationship.

COMMON WISDOM

Early in a relationship, as couples profess their love and discuss their future together, they explicitly and implicitly promise such things as mutual commitment, support, and care for each other. In healthy relationships, the unspoken contract closely reflects the conscious, spoken agreements the couple makes. These agreements are generally influenced by common wisdom we receive from our elders, spiritual leaders, and mental health experts.

From the time we are teenagers and start thinking about choosing a life partner, we are told that strong relationships are the result of hard work and involve things like compassion, forgiveness, and compromise. We are advised to accept our partner's faults and take responsibility for our own. Wise people tell us that it takes time to learn how to live together, to negotiate differences, and to communicate in the context of an intimate relationship.

Therefore, we are encouraged to stay committed and work through the hard times with the idea that we will be rewarded with a happier relationship in the end. *Unfortunately, the very teachings that create a roadmap for a healthy relationship when both partners participate in them can actually put the abused partner at a severe disadvantage in an abusive situation.* Let's look at these principles and see how they are applied in both healthy and abusive relationship dynamics.

PRACTICE COMPASSION AND EMPATHY

The idea that couples will connect through empathic and loving gestures is an example of a widely held, but usually unspoken, aspect of a healthy relationship contract. Showing compassion, accepting others as they are, and being forgiving are all ways to say, "I love you. I care about you. I'll be there for you." They create an environment of emotional safety that gives people room to be imperfect, to have times of weakness and vulnerability and still feel loved, reassured, and supported.

Emotionally abused partners anticipate sharing those kinds of interactions with their loved one. But, to their dismay they find that abusers can't or won't engage with them empathically, at least not for very long. Chloe describes the difference between abusive and compassionate responses from her partners:

> In my old relationship, if I brought something up to my ex that bothered me, "I'm upset." He would say something like, "Oh, you're being dramatic. You're being too sensitive. You're being crazy. You're being annoying."
>
> But in this new healthy relationship, my partner has never said that to me. Not one time, even if I am being annoying. If I am getting under his skin for whatever reason, he doesn't say that. When I say, "I'm upset." He will say, "Why? What is going on?"
>
> And there are times when I can be upset, and he may not understand why. He just can't wrap his head around it. But he doesn't say, "That is stupid." He says, "I don't understand why you're upset, but I'm upset that you are upset, so I want to help you." We don't think the same, so what I understand he may not understand, but you don't have to understand the issue to empathize and understand that your partner is upset.

When people feel understood and accepted by their significant other, it not only creates a closer, more intimate relationship, but it also helps people feel stronger and more confident as individuals.[4]

In contrast, regularly dismissing and shaming a partner and consistently refusing to be there for them when they reach out in vulnerability are abusive acts because, in addition to undermining the health of the relationship, they diminish and devalue the other person.

GIVING AND RECEIVING COMPASSION

It is not that caring partners always get things right; they don't. There are times when people misunderstand their partner's needs, fail to be there the way the other would like, or just have moments of thoughtlessness. But most couples can talk about what doesn't work and come to a better understanding of each other as the relationship progresses. In the big picture, loving couples are consistently there for each other, whereas abusive relationships are consistently one-sided:

> *When I show him compassion, he shows me compassion as well. It is a mutual thing. It is not just something that I am constantly giving that I am not receiving.*

> —Becca

Most people want to give compassion as well as receive it. There is a certain kind of joy that comes from showing care in a way that connects with a loved one. We receive from giving. Samantha had this to say about her new partner:

> *Then I met somebody who is able to receive the love I want to pour out. It's so nice.*

Abusers not only fail to show compassion, but they also seem incapable of receiving it in a way that makes a heartfelt connection. Vincent expressed his frustration and distress when his attempts at being supportive with his wife did not reach her in the loving way he intended:

> *I just assumed that if you work hard at it, be compassionate, give and give and give, you could make anything work. That may be true with some people, but not with my wife.*

A sense of dismay and frustration is not unusual for people who are committed to sharing a relationship based on care and compassion with a partner who cannot or will not meet them in that place, in either the giving or the receiving.

THE PARTNER'S SIDE OF THE CONTRACT

As abused people try to make sense of their loved one's hurtful behaviors, they put a lot of effort into understanding them and figuring out how to respond in supportive ways:

> *I tried to figure out, where does this rage come from? Did something happen when he was in the Marines? Did something happen when he was growing up? I could never figure out where all that rage was coming from. And I was trying to make sense of it so I could have some compassion for him.*
>
> —ALICE

It is not unusual for partners to look at the abuser's hurtful behaviors compassionately and see a wounded soul in need of healing. They believe that loving responses such as understanding, support, kindness, and patience will heal their loved one's deep emotional wounds. In theory, they are not wrong. It is well documented that empathy, validation, and an unconditional positive attitude toward a person create a healing environment for them.[5] But in practice, abusers are not healed by their partner's care and understanding. On the contrary, the hurtful behaviors get worse because from the abuser's perspective it looks like the partner is agreeing to the mistreatment:

> *It happened because I kept trying to fix it. I wanted to make things better, but whatever I did didn't work. All the things you think should work didn't work. Looking back, I think that the more I accepted that type of behavior, the more it happened. It just kept getting worse and worse.*
>
> —CQ

Similarly, trying to live by the "accept others as they are" principle in an abusive relationship frequently leads partners to accept increasingly unacceptable behaviors:

> *I would get to the point sometimes when I would be really hurt, almost in tears, and I would leave. I'd be walking down the street thinking, "It's just him. Don't be so upset about it. That's how he is. Everything will be fine when you go back. Don't worry about it. If I'm going to love him and be with him, I have to accept him for who he is."*
>
> —WARREN

Another person, Ellen, gained a new perspective when she realized that accepting people as they are does not include accepting ongoing hurtful behaviors:

> *It was very much a belief system for me that if you truly love someone you wouldn't hurt them. It took me a long time to flip it around to: "If you loved me, you wouldn't hurt me."*

In abusive relationships, there is not a mutual exchange of care and compassion. Abused partners are focused on making compassion a cornerstone of the relationship while abusers have difficulty both showing compassion consistently and receiving it as the loving, healing gift their partner intends it to be.

THE ABUSER'S SIDE OF THE CONTRACT

Although there are times when abusers show a caring side, they habitually take a self-serving approach to the relationship.

Often, they are simply so self-absorbed that they are oblivious to, or unconcerned about, their significant other's needs and concerns. Consequently, they don't respond empathically when their partners reach out to them. Most abusers go further than a lack of compassion, however. They often will take a hostile attitude and engage in put-downs, name-calling, and other demeaning behaviors that shock, wound, and confuse their partners. Beyond that, as abusers seek ever-expanding power and control, many will actively work to undermine their partner's strengths and exploit their weaknesses.

Undermining Strengths

People in loving relationships desire their partner's happiness, so they cheer on the other's aspirations and celebrate their achievements. Whereas many abusers will either shrewdly or openly undercut their partner's dreams and successes:

> I loved that job. Loved it. He would say things like they are overworking you. They don't believe in what you are saying. I would tell him stories about what was going on at work, and he would find negatives in it and make me feel like they were taking advantage of me. Then I started believing it to the point where I ended up leaving.

> *My current partner believes in me. He doesn't second-guess*
> *me all the time. So that helps my confidence. He encourages*
> *me. He values my profession.*
>
> —Sierra

In addition to diminishing what their partner does, abusers will strike at the core of who their partner is. While most couples express appreciation for the other's positive qualities, abusers will find a way to belittle them. Eaglin explains how her ex-husband used her positive self-concept against her:

> *Of all the things in the world I don't want to be, it's selfish.*
> *That just makes me sad. I'd rather share. I'm an identical*
> *twin. We would share the Skittles to the last Skittle, and it*
> *felt better splitting the last Skittle than not sharing. That is*
> *what feels natural to me.*

Her abusive partner manipulated her by constantly telling her she was selfish: for forgetting something at the grocery store, for letting the pan soak while she ate breakfast, for spending time with her twin sister, even selfish when she ordered food for herself that he didn't approve of:

> *If I ordered a salad at a restaurant or for takeout, I was spend-*
> *ing money in a selfish way. And he would say how selfish I*
> *was. I was spoiled and I could just make a salad at home. So,*
> *I stopped ordering salads. I wasn't just doing things wrong,*
> *but selfishly.*

Exploiting Weaknesses

Besides undercutting their partner's positive sense of self, the abuser also will exploit their weaknesses. For example, magnifying the anxieties of someone who has a fear of going out by "compassionately" reminding them how hard it is for them to cope. Or pointing out to someone who was adopted that their birth mother didn't want them and zeroing in on problems with their adoptive family to "prove" that they don't value them, either. Or telling their partner who has a history of a weak immune system that they should "stay safe at home" even when they are well enough to go out.

Another tactic is criticizing, ridiculing, and/or sabotaging the first steps of someone who is trying to overcome their fears. For instance, Sierra, who has a history of anorexia, describes how her ex-husband used her vulnerability to demean her. He encouraged poor eating habits, shamed her when she wanted to go to the gym, and reinforced her tendency to have a negative body image:

> I would verbalize to him, "Oh, my God. I feel so fat." And he would say, "Yeah, you've gained a lot of weight." He would pinch my stomach. My stomach was really flat in the beginning, and he would pinch it. I would tell him to stop. I felt like the doughboy.

Fortunately for her, she remarried, and her current husband gives her the support that people in a loving relationship can expect:

> My husband doesn't comment about my stuff. He knows that eating is sensitive to me. He is very encouraging. Completely. He respects anything I do. He doesn't question me.

Abused partners don't often get that kind of empathy and support. Here is a typical refrain of people in abusive relationships:

> There was no sympathy. No empathy. When I told him how I was feeling, it didn't matter. He was very good at showing

me that he couldn't care less about anything that concerned
me, and that hurt me more than anything else. And then
when he'd feel like I was kind of realizing all that, he would
pull me back in a little bit.

—DENISE

When an abused partner becomes so upset that the abuser fears
they are losing control over the situation, the abuser may apologize
and show enough care to entice their partner back in. These shows of
kindness and apparent reconciliation give abused people false hope.
It leads them to believe the abusive behaviors are just a rough patch
that the couple can work through.

THE PARTNER'S INTENTION VS.
THE ABUSER'S INTERPRETATION

It is often a painful and frustrating mystery to abused partners
why their efforts at offering care and compassion don't result in a
more loving partnership. That is because while most people see those
things as part of a healthy relationship contract, *abusers see them as*
acceptance of the abuse and permission to keep abusing. When viewed
from the abuser's side of the contract, they look like positive rein-
forcement for negative behaviors, so the hurtfulness continues and
increases over time.

After spending some time in therapy, Chloe got a clearer idea of
what was really happening between her and her abusive ex-husband.
She explains the mismatch in their relationship contract this way:

He literally said to me one time, "I know that you love me,
and I know that I can do and say whatever, because you'll
always be here. It doesn't matter what I do. You'll come back."
That was hurtful, but in a way, my self-esteem was so bad,

and my idea of love was so warped that I was proud that he said it because it meant that I was showing him unconditional love. He was calling me a doormat and saying, "I can walk all over you, and you will still be there."

That is a stark and shocking example of how the relationship contract plays out in the twisted world of emotional abuse. Although it is the basic blueprint for emotionally abusive relationships, few abusers reveal their side of the contract so openly. Most are much more subtle and mix in just enough kindness and caring to keep their partner believing that they really do share the same loving contract.

COMPROMISE AND BE CONSIDERATE

Compromise is another piece of common wisdom that supports a healthy partnership. One of the joys of relationship is being a source of happiness for each other. It is one reason why couples are willing to make some sacrifices for the other person's sake. This gift of self is another unspoken part of a healthy relationship contract. But an abused person's attempts to compromise and be considerate are often manipulated by abusers who consistently prioritize their own wants and needs at the expense of their partner's. Samantha describes her experience with a supportive partner after leaving an abusive one:

> *To my ex-husband, I was an annoyance, a burden, and a bother. I was an obstacle to get around. And that is a very lonely feeling. The comparison is, now I'm married to a man who considers me. He considers how things make me feel, how his behavior affects me. The other thing that's different is we are doing it together, and we feel like a team.*

Like people in healthy relationships, abused partners anticipate that mutual consideration and compromise will form a kind of team-like connection with their partner, but then they find they are regularly mired in power struggles instead.

That can be another point of confusion in discerning between healthy and abusive relationships because most couples do have power struggles from time to time as they sort out how to manage their individual wants and needs. In fact, when people are in mutually respectful relationships the process of debating how to negotiate differences helps couples build stronger partnerships in the long run. It allows each person to assert their preferences, boundaries, and individuality. With honest and open communication, each person knows where the other stands. This is the starting point for productive compromise.

Abusers sabotage the compromise process to ensure that the relationship works on their terms and for their benefit. Any consideration of the partner is secondary, at best.

MUTUAL CARE VS. ONE-SIDEDNESS

When one part of a couple is living by the common wisdom that compromise and consideration are part of a healthy relationship, and the other person is living by a code of self-interest, the balance of give and take gets skewed:

> *I was fine with him going out and doing stuff. What I wasn't fine with was that it wasn't reciprocated, like, "I've been going out a lot lately. Did you want to go do something? I'll take care of the kids." And I'm not saying it's his job to notice that, but he didn't support me doing what I wanted because it cost money, or he would have to deal with the kids. So I didn't have that kind of freedom.*
>
> —SAMANTHA

It is not uncommon for both people, even in strong partnerships, to sometimes feel like they are giving more than their share, but reciprocity in a healthy relationship is not about keeping an even score. The give and take of compromise keep a balanced flow going so each partner receives enough care and consideration overall that they can continue giving without feeling depleted or resentful. That doesn't happen in abusive relationships:

> *There was no reciprocity. When you are repeatedly prioritizing the relationship and they aren't, that takes a toll.*
>
> —ABIGAIL

And the toll it takes goes beyond an imbalance of give and take. Compromise, cooperation, and consideration are among the ways supportive couples express love and respect for each other:

> *My current relationship is not hard work at all. It's mutually respectful. We discuss our wants and needs. My husband can take feedback and will make changes if I ask. He is willing to do what he can to make me happy and to ensure the relationship is healthy. I don't feel so much of a weight on my shoulders. I feel like he helps me carry everything in our relationship. I'm not carrying it by myself.*
>
> —BECCA

When a person refuses to offer care and consideration to their partner, it communicates a disregard that diminishes and devalues them.

HOW ABUSERS AVOID COMPROMISING

Compromise usually begins when one person brings up a complaint or an issue that requires cooperation from the partner. At that point, most couples have a talk to figure out a solution together. Even in compatible relationships, if one partner asks the other to make a change, there may be some defensiveness and resistance. The key is that they have a two-way communication about the issue.

Refusing to Talk About It

In abusive relationships, however, the road to compromise is often blocked at the very beginning because abusers simply refuse to discuss the matter:

> *Most anytime I wanted to talk about anything, like maybe I'm worried about money, or I wish we had more together*

time, or I don't think you're spending enough time with the
baby, he would either say: "I don't want to talk about this
right now," or "This is stressing me out," or "I don't know
what you're talking about," or "Why would you say that?"

—CHLOE

It is impossible to reach a compromise with someone who refuses to acknowledge an issue and engage in a conversation about it. People who don't realize they are in a relationship with an abuser often wonder if they didn't communicate clearly or if their request really was unreasonable. And most abusers are such good manipulators they can steer the conversation so far afield that their partner has no idea what they are talking about or how they got there. Furthermore, many abusers respond to requests by going on the offense and listing their partner's faults and failings in order to justify not cooperating. Consequently, partners are left frustrated and confused and, most importantly, the original issue goes unaddressed.

Ignoring Agreements

Another tactic abusers use to avoid compromising is to agree to something, then not follow through:

I kept on trying to talk to him, to find another way to con-
nect with him. Let's read this book together. Let's go to this
therapist. Let's go away for a weekend. I kept on doing that
kind of stuff, and he would buy into it to a certain extent
then just not do it.

—JAYLA

This scenario could play out with any number of issues such as how to manage chores, money, or childcare. Sometimes abusers deny that there ever was such an agreement. Other times, they respond with excuses, rationalizations, and promises to do better in the future, keeping their partner hoping for better times. While most people drop the ball occasionally, abusers regularly fail to follow through on promises and agreements.

Making Excuses

Here's an example of how an abuser may listen to their partner's concerns, find an excuse for refusing to cooperate, and do what they want regardless of their partner's genuine needs:

> *With my ex-husband, we were always on opposite ends. If I won, he lost. When I had the second baby, I asked him to take paternity leave to give me some help. "No, I can't. I have too much work." Then later I was emptying a trash can and found three movie ticket stubs for matinees that month.*
>
> —SAMANTHA

When Samantha asked for help, her husband didn't come back with a compromise, such as, "Well, I can't take that much time off, but I could take this much time." He did what he wanted for himself and covered his disregard for her by using work as an excuse. When one partner sees the relationship in terms of a competition with winners and losers, and the other partner sees it in terms of mutual care and consideration, the non-competitive partner is going to lose over and over again.

Sabotaging Plans

Sometimes abusers hide their disregard for their partners by agreeing to a compromise, then sabotaging it:

So he might agree to go see my family for Christmas or some-thing, but he would sit on the couch the whole time, and not interact with anybody. Then he would always conveniently have a stomachache. "I don't feel good. We should leave soon."

When we would leave, he would say, "See, this is why I don't want to go. Your family doesn't like me."

I'd say, "You were looking at your phone the whole time."

He'd say, "You know I feel awkward around people."

Then I would feel guilty that I made him go to a family thing that made him feel so uncomfortable, so I probably wouldn't talk to my family for a while, and we didn't have to go back.

—CHLOE

This abuser gave his wife the illusion he was willing to compro-mise, but then made the situation so awkward that he was able to con-vince her she was asking too much of him. He took advantage of her concern for his comfort to manipulate her out of something that was important to her. While loving partners regularly take steps to make sure the relationship is working for the couple, abusers regularly take steps to make sure the relationship is working only for themselves.

HOW ABUSED PARTNERS BECOME COMPROMISED

Their genuine desire to see their partners happy, the idea that compromise is part of a healthy relationship, and a commitment to doing what it takes to make the relationship work, all set people up to be taken advantage of by abusers:

I work from home. I am a useful kind of guy, so I would do the laundry, pick up some groceries, shuttle both kids, take care of the dogs, cook dinner so it was ready to reheat. Instead of noticing any of that, she would complain that the floors weren't swept. But the next day if I swept the floors, the big problem was that the laundry wasn't done. She constantly told me, in ways large and small, that I was wrong. I was wrong about the groceries, wrong about the dogs, wrong about the cleaning. Any questioning to the "you're wrong" was met with emotional and verbal attacks, so to keep the peace, I'd just let it all roll past and would emerge unscathed. Of course, it wasn't rolling past me completely because just listening to it was damaging.

—Vincent

Refusing to be pleased is an abusive ploy. The tactic is, "The less I am pleased with what they do, the harder they will try to please me." While the partner is focused on an exchange of thoughtfulness and consideration, the abuser is focused on gaining power and control over their partner.

In the fog of emotional abuse, people can lose sight of where a reasonable line for compromise is, and they end up giving away too much. Warren shares how he tried to ease the worries of his highly jealous partner:

When we went out with new people, I would totally ignore them. I was almost rude to them, because I didn't want him to see me talking to them. Then we would get home and he would say, "You have something going on with him, don't you? Why weren't you talking to him? It was almost like you were afraid if you talked to him, I would see that there was something going on." And he would even tell people, "Warren is very standoffish and rude," and that is not who I am. I was being that way for him.

Ultimately, Warren compromised his own way of being in the world in an effort to make his partner happy. Even then the abuser wouldn't be satisfied because what he really wanted was to demean and dominate his partner.

Eventually, without realizing it, abused partners begin to go beyond compromising about issues and begin to compromise themselves. Becca looked back on her abusive marriage and concluded:

> *Compromising my standards is not the same thing as compromising in coming to an agreement. I was compromising my standards and my worth as a person. You shouldn't have to compromise your worth, you know? I understand compromising on what time we'll eat dinner, or if we'll sit at the table, but not my worth.*

Another abused partner quipped:

> *What life with an abuser has taught me is that when you sacrifice yourself, what you get is a sacrificed self. Nobody is happier, nobody is healed, nothing is better.*
>
> —TERRI

It usually takes therapy and time away from the abuser to gain that kind of clarity. Amid the manipulation and confusion that is emotional abuse, it can be very difficult to get a clear picture of what is going on.

THE ABUSER'S GIVE AND TAKE

Another thing that makes it hard to discern emotional abuse is that there are usually times in the relationship when things go well. For instance, it can look like abusers are compromising when they give in on things that don't matter to them. Or if it serves their self-interest to be thoughtful and giving, they will do that. For example, if abusers think they are losing their grip on their partner, if they want to impress other people, or if they simply want to bolster their own self-image, they can be generous and indulgent. When things go well in an abusive relationship, they go well because they are going the way the abuser wants them to:

> *We were friends. We had a good time hanging out as long as I did everything he wanted. And I am pretty easygoing and laid-back, so I just kind of gave in on everything. It was only when I wanted to do something he didn't like, or if I challenged him that we had a problem.*
>
> —SIERRA

When things don't go the way emotional abusers want, they often become manipulative, resistant, or verbally aggressive in order to maintain or regain power and control:

> *If I wanted to do something and it wasn't something he wanted me to do, he would say, "That's stupid. Why would you want to do that? Why would you even think about doing that?"*
>
> —SIERRA

Or, even more aggressively:

> *We were at a store, and I saw a teddy bear they were selling for a charity benefit. I picked it up and he goes, "We don't need that bear." He went to get the car and said, "When I come back, you better not have that bear in your hand." I thought, "Wow, he's threatening me." I bought the bear, and when he came back, he yelled, "You better put that goddamn*

bear down! You cannot buy that bear!" It was totally like a father-child situation. He chewed me out.

—SIERRA

In the give and take of relationship, abusers do a lot of the taking and just enough giving to confuse the picture.

TAKE RESPONSIBILITY FOR
YOUR PART OF THE PROBLEM

In strong partnerships, *both* people are willing to look at how they might be contributing to any problems, and *both* are willing to make adjustments for the sake of their partner and the relationship. It is never easy to take criticism, but listening to a partner's concerns and then honestly considering if these changes are warranted is something emotionally mature people do.

In mutually respectful relationships where each person has the other's best interest at heart as well as their own, constructive criticism can inspire individual growth and improve partnerships. Because emotionally abused people believe they share that kind of relationship contract, they trust that their partner's complaints are well intentioned:

> *Anytime I would try to approach him, it was, "Why can't you let things go? You're too needy. You're too judgmental. You have unrealistic expectations. You think life is supposed to be a romantic comedy—reality is not like that." Then, after all the years of hearing that, I thought, well, maybe I am the problem. Maybe I can fix this.*
>
> —CQ

When partners trust the abuser's negative (and often untrue) assessments and change their behavior in the belief that they are taking responsibility for their part of the problem, they are actually in the process of adapting to the abuse. For example, when an abused person repeatedly hears things like, "You're too demanding, too judgmental, too selfish," and consequently tries to be more patient, more understanding, more selfless, they are beginning to shift into the abuser's relationship contract in which more and more is expected of the partner, while less and less is expected of the abuser. This example clearly demonstrates how differently the two partners in emotionally abusive relationships approach taking responsibility:

> *When I came to him with a problem, he would say, "This is too much. You're too sensitive. You're being overbearing. You're hard to be with." Then I felt guilty. "Oh, no! I am too much. I am being negative. Oh, my God, I'm making it hard for him." So then I started looking up effective ways to communicate so I wouldn't be hurting him.*
>
> —CHLOE

Typical of emotional abusers, this man successfully derailed his partner's complaint by deflecting. He blamed her for the very concern she brought up. She then turned her focus to how she could change to fix her side of the problem. Her original issue never got addressed, and the abuser didn't make any effort toward caring for his partner or improving the relationship.

In abusive partnerships, the abuser regularly denies responsibility for problems, refuses to make changes, and blames their partner. Meanwhile, the abused person regularly listens to their partner's complaint, invests a lot of time trying to figure out what their part of the problem might be, and explores what they can do to improve things. Consequently, the abused partner ends up carrying an inordinate amount of responsibility for the well-being of the relationship:

> *I took a lot of responsibility for the relationship. If it didn't go well, I thought it was my fault, because he did blame me for everything, so I took on ownership of everything. I went to individual therapy to work on myself. He wouldn't go to couples counseling when I brought it up. He never worked on self-development or change. He saw that he did no wrong.*
>
> —SIERRA

Even when abusers are not directly blaming them, partners tend to respond to the distress they feel in the relationship with self-examination. Like any person who understands the concept of personal responsibility, they look at their own behavior in an honest attempt to see how they may be contributing to the problem:

> *I used to always question things. Every time I would start to think, "Am I a victim here?" Then I'd think, "Well, sometimes a victim brings things on. Did I bring something on? And what did I do? Maybe I need to re-evaluate myself." I was thinking that more than re-evaluating him.*
>
> —WARREN

Other typical self-reflective questions partners ask include:

- What faults am I bringing to this problem?

- Do I take things the wrong way? Am I being overly sensitive?

- Are there experiences in my past that would make me inclined to see injury or issues where there are none?

- How can I do things differently to get a better reaction?

- Am I being unreasonable? Judgmental? Unfair? Bossy?

- How do I need to change?

The partner's tendency for self-examination is reinforced by common wisdom offered from respected sources, including the mental health profession. For instance, Samantha (and many other people) found Al-Anon to be immensely helpful in the healing process, but she did have one caveat for people in emotionally abusive relationships:

Here is the problem with going to Al-Anon, because in Al-Anon, rightfully so, you're supposed to keep the focus on yourself and not complain. We just talk about us. We just focus on how we can change. So I was super focused on that for years. How am I going to change? How am I going to be able to live with this? What can I do to let it go? But honestly, it just got worse, which I didn't understand why because it seemed like he was getting what he wanted.

It gets worse because the interplay of the two different relationship contracts serves the abuser well. In emotional abuse, the combination of "take responsibility for your part of the problem" and "don't judge others" mixed with the abusers' habit of refusing responsibility and blaming their partner sets up the one-sidedness that is the hallmark of abusive partnerships.

There is a crucial line to draw between acceptance, forgiveness, and self-improvement vs. tolerating verbal and psychological abuse, and staying in a situation that is harmful and slowly but steadily wearing down your self-esteem, eroding your personal empowerment, and sapping your energy.

STAY COMMITTED

The idea of being committed to a life partner and the shared relationship is a piece of common wisdom that helps people weather the difficulties most couples face. Many people are not just committed to their partners, however. They are also committed to living by relationship principles such as: be compassionate, forgive, take responsibility for your part of the problem, accept others as they are, and don't be a quitter. This sense of commitment leads abused people to stay with toxic partners in the belief that if they keep trying to work it out, things will get better:

> *I made a promise to her. We were engaged, dear God. I made a promise that I was going to love her no matter what, so I felt like unconditional love brought about more responsibility. I truly believed that if I did everything I could, then we would succeed, but again, it was very much one-sided.*
>
> —Ellen

The idea of being committed to a life partner is also an enduring social value that is passed on from generation to generation:

> *I believe in the institution of marriage. And we're not supposed to just give up. We are supposed to work through our differences. As did my parents, whether they were good or bad, and I believe that with all my heart.*
>
> —Belinda

In addition to a value extolled by family elders and society at large, commitment in relationships is also a spiritual value. Spiritual or religious teachings are a strong force in many people's lives and are not easily discarded:

*Those kinds of principles: compassion, compromise, and for-
giveness remind me of the core training of religious paths
about those things. I think that would be another reason why
I worked so hard to stay in relationship. The religious teaching about how you're supposed to be in relationship. Those
seeds were planted very deeply for me.*

—ABIGAIL

For many people, being committed to their partner and the relationship is a matter of morality and character, so deciding to leave
involves a struggle with their conscience:

*When I was unhappy enough to think of leaving, I needed
to grapple with my belief system and self-judgment about
wanting to leave, and possible judgment from friends, family, children, and my religious community. There is the belief
that relationships fail because people aren't doing the work,
so that means do the work.*

— ABIGAIL

Even after people have left the religious institutions where they
learned these principles, they may still hold onto the idea that being
committed to a life partner is a value to be honored:

*I am not as religious as I have been in the past, but there is
the sense of if I was just better at forgiveness, and letting go of
things, and being patient, and letting people be who they are,
all of those things, that it wasn't just a good way of being; it
was also a more spiritual or religious way of being, a kinder
way of being, so that impacted my belief system.*

— ABIGAIL

These teachings are so powerful that even people who have been rejected by their religious institution are still guided by them. Jacob, a gay man, explained how the values he learned at church stayed with him, even after the church rejected him:

> *Even after I came to the realization that I needed to leave, my spiritual programming—I didn't believe in divorce, and I was committed to this person—compelled me to stay and make it work. And so even though that whole idea system had shunned me and threw me out, I still carried it forward into this relationship. And that was one of the reasons I stayed as long as I did.*

Whether people come from a spiritual or secular orientation, whether they took formal vows or not, and whether they legally married or not, most feel a deep sense of commitment to their chosen life partner. Consequently, they will invest a lot of time and effort—months, years, even decades—honoring that commitment and doing everything they can to make their relationship a success.

BE FORGIVING

Even in loving relationships, people sometimes hurt each other. The common wisdom to be forgiving opens the door for caring partners to make amends and repair hurts. They can learn from their mistakes and ultimately create a stronger relationship built on deeper understanding of the other person.

The first step in a true apology is to acknowledge that an offense has occurred. Abusers often dodge this step by ignoring that they have hurt their partner. If they do acknowledge doing harm, they frequently minimize what they have done, make excuses, or try to cast part or all of the blame on the partner. Or they may offer a pseudo apology such as, "I'm sorry you got your feelings hurt" or "I'm sorry you feel that way." Since the offender is not taking responsibility for their actions, there is no real apology:

> *There is no accountability in an abusive relationship. I would forgive him and then he would just turn around and do it again. So when you continue to try and forgive this act and then that act, it just goes nowhere.*
>
> —ALICE

Importantly, apologies include the expectation that the offending person will stop the hurtful behaviors. Abusers rarely do that. Though abusers sometimes apologize, the abuses return before long:

> *My ex would say, "I'm sorry." And my definition of "I'm sorry" is he's not going to do the behavior again. His definition of sorry is not that. Then it got to the point where I'd say, "Look, you keep doing this," and he would fall back on, "I don't know why I do it." Kind of little boyish and not taking responsibility. So then I would feel like I had to give him*

*room to grow, or give him another chance, because he's try-
ing. I don't know about forgiveness so much, but when he
said, "Sorry," I equated that with he's truly sorry, so if he is
truly contrite, I'm not going to hold that against him. That
was my philosophy.*

—Samantha

In the beginning, people trust the apologies. They believe their
partner truly wants to make things better. There is hope that the
hurtfulness will end, and their relationship will improve. Eventually,
though, they see that that is not going to happen with an abuser:

*At first especially, when he finally came and said I'm sorry, I
felt that melting of the anger.*

"I'm sorry."

"Oh, I'm sorry, too."

"I'll do better."

"Oh, me too."

*And then by the thousandth time, you don't believe the words
anymore and you don't believe they're sorry anymore.*

—Anika

An abuser's apology is not motivated by remorse and a willingness to change as much as it is motivated by a desire to temporarily
restore equilibrium in the relationship. In other words, it is about
the abuser's comfort level. An abuser's apology is an attempt to make
things okay *with* their partner in the moment, not *for* their partner
in the long run.

GOOD ADVICE GOES WRONG

Having compassion, being forgiving, and making some compromises and sacrifices for the sake of a relationship are not wrong. Neither are taking responsibility for one's part of the problem, accepting others as they are, and being committed to working through difficulties. In fact, it is hard to imagine a healthy relationship without those elements. That is what makes emotional abuse so confusing, frustrating, and discouraging, because *what works in creating a healthy relationship usually makes things worse for the abused partner in an abusive relationship.*

Abusers are unwilling or unable to engage in an equal partnership based on the elements of common wisdom. Instead, they meet their own need for power and control by taking advantage of their partner's efforts to create such a relationship.

It takes two people to make a relationship a success, but it only takes one to make it fail.

SUMMARY

- In emotionally abusive partnerships, there is an unconscious and unequal relationship contract that benefits the abuser and harms the abused partner.

- Emotionally abused partners strive for mutual respect and consideration without realizing that their partner is striving for power and control.

- The common wisdom that guides healthy relationships works against the abused partner in the context of emotional abuse.

Practice Compassion and Empathy

- Abused people habitually show empathy and compassion for their partners.

- Although abusers sometimes show a caring side, they regularly show disregard and disdain for their partners.

- Abusers interpret compassion and understanding as acceptance of the abuse and permission to keep abusing.

Compromise and Consideration

- Abusers avoid compromising by refusing to talk about issues, sabotaging the process, or failing to follow through on agreements.

- In an effort to be thoughtful or to make the relationship work, abused partners often go beyond making compromises to compromising themselves.

Take Responsibility for Your Part of the Problem

- Abused partners tend to take responsibility not only for their own actions, but also for the success of the relationship.

- Abusers dodge responsibility for their hurtful actions by deflecting responsibility onto their partners instead.

- Consequently, both the abuser and the abused partner focus on how the abused person may be at fault in the relationship, while the abuser takes little or no responsibility.

Stay Committed

- Many people stay in abusive relationships not only out of a sense of commitment to their partner, but also out of a commitment to their core values.

- Many abused partners believe if they just stay committed and keep working on the relationship, things will get better.

Be Forgiving

- In a true apology, the offender acknowledges that they have harmed another. Emotional abusers usually ignore that they have done something hurtful.

- In emotionally abusive relationships, apologies and forgiveness rarely, if ever, end the abusive behaviors.

ACTIVITY

1. Do you believe that empathy, compassion, and love will heal your partner so they will no longer feel the need to do hurtful things? If so, what has their response to your

empathy and compassion been so far? Have they become less or more abusive over time?

2. When you approach your partner for a compromise or cooperation, do they genuinely hear your requests? Are your concerns productively resolved most of the time? If not, what happens?

3. Do you spend a lot of time exploring your own behavior looking for things you can do differently to make the relationship better? What have you tried? What was the outcome?

4. What do you think of the "love thyself" part of the "Love thy neighbor as thyself" teaching?

5. Does your partner have a hard time apologizing when they have been hurtful? Do they engage in the same hurtful behaviors no matter how many times they have apologized?

6. Do you believe that if you just keep trying the relationship will eventually get better? How long have you been trying? Has it gotten better overall?

IS IT SUPPOSED TO BE THIS HARD?

No. In healthy relationships, both people regularly show compassion and empathy for their partners. They both make a habit of being considerate and making compromises for the sake of the other person and the health of the relationship. When they have hurt their partner, they not only apologize, but they also take ownership and responsibility for their part of the problem and make real efforts to stop the hurtful behaviors. Sierra makes this important point:

> *Abuse is not a lack of compatibility. It's the abusive person's lack of wanting to actually understand who you are and wanting to actually honor what your needs are.*

CHAPTER 3

TRUST AND THE EVER-CHANGING CONTRACT

"Why Is This So Hard?"

*I believed him. There were plenty of other people who did,
too. I believed that he was this patient, loving, thoughtful
guy, and I felt like I hung the moon in his eyes. I believed
him when he said I had an insatiable need for conversation,
so conversations were rare. I believed him when he said I was
an immature child who needed more than was appropriate,
so I didn't ask for much. All these parts of myself I used to be
clear on, like being friendly and social, but then I believed
I was imposing and selfish.*

—EAGLIN

If you are emotionally abused, you may recognize yourself in Eaglin's experience. Did you, like her, begin your relationship believing that your beloved was an emotionally trustworthy person? Did your loved one give you reason to believe that they valued and cherished you? Because you trusted them, did you also believe them when they began to slip in negative messages about you? Over time, did their negativity toward you diminish your belief in yourself?

RELATIONSHIP TRUST

In addition to common wisdom, trust is another element of healthy relationships that creates a liability for abused partners. When people think about trust between couples, they usually focus on things like fidelity and keeping promises. However, there are other aspects of relationship trust that are so much a part of human nature that they are assumed and felt rather than clearly recognized.

Humans have an inborn need to form deep emotional bonds with someone who values them and can be trusted to offer emotional safety, care, and support on a regular basis.[6] This need is so essential that when people receive it, their well-being is embellished, but when deprived of it, their physical and mental health suffers.[7] Common wisdom about relationships has been passed down through generations because it encourages an emotionally safe environment in which people can make those connections. This basic human need to connect with a trusted loved one forms another layer in the unspoken relationship contract.

ABUSERS VIOLATE
BASIC RELATIONSHIP TRUST

Trust involves a belief in the good intentions of the other. It includes a sense of being safe, valued, and cared for by the partner, and by its very nature leads to vulnerability. The heart of a healthy relationship contract is the idea that each person will honor and safeguard the trust and vulnerability of their partner. It is a sacred compact because it gives the trusted individual a unique power to either nurture or injure their partner at a profoundly deep level. In abusive relationships, abused partners give their beloved the trust a loving relationship contract calls for, and abusers repeatedly violate that trust:

> One of the big realizations for me after exiting the relationship was that I was having an intimate relationship, but I'm

not so sure he was. What I mean by that is I would confide in him about my fears, and my worries, and my own beliefs about my own shortcomings, and he never did. He never said anything about himself that he would consider worrisome. And I realized he never confided anything like that to me. I don't know how I missed that. As a result, he had all this ammunition to use against me at the end of the marriage.

—KENNEDY

Humans get into relationships not only because they love and value their partners, but also because they feel loved and valued by them. So, when a loved one says undercutting or disparaging things to their significant other, it constitutes a serious betrayal of trust. A person close to one's heart can wound like no other:

I was sad, very sad. Crushed. This is someone I respected so much, and he is telling me I'm a bad person, so I was crushed and scared. I felt bad about myself. There were times when I wanted to kill myself.

—JACKIE

When partners trust that the abuser is an emotionally safe person, they are vulnerable to manipulation and mistreatment.

REFUSING TO CONNECT
VIOLATES RELATIONSHIP TRUST

One of the primary reasons people enter intimate relationships is to have a loving connection with their partner. So, when one person consistently rejects the other's efforts to connect by ignoring, withdrawing, or stonewalling, it denies a basic human need that is the foundation of intimate partnerships. Jayla describes how her husband's repeated rejections affected her:

He would walk in a room and not acknowledge me, not look at me. That was very common. "You are not even worthwhile enough to look at." I was very depressed. At one time I was suicidal. I would be angry most of the time, and of course that didn't help. I tried everything. I tried being sweet. I tried being sexy. I tried being funny—anything to try to make us work. I felt even less confident in myself. It happened over all those years, and if my own husband doesn't want to spend time with me, there must be something wrong with me.

Although it is not a partner's job to be in service to the other's ego and self-esteem, how loved ones treat each other has a major impact on their sense of self. Ongoing rejection and disregard from her ex led Jayla to despair and the brink of suicide. By contrast, her current partner's care and high regard for her supports her sense of well-being:

Then I met the man I am engaged to, and he is entirely different. He treats me like a queen. I found it hard to be able to trust him in the beginning, but he was very willing to talk. We've gone over the same conversation many, many times. He says, "This is who I am. I like being with you. That's not going to change." Not only does he say it, but he also does it. He makes time for me and shows me that I am important to him.

For people who have been in abusive relationships, part of the hard work in a new relationship is taking the risk to trust again.

Abusers also avoid connecting lovingly with their partners by sabotaging conversations, attempts at intimacy, and other efforts to reach out. Jayla continues:

I would tell him what would make me feel good, like I would say, "Why don't you just invite me to lunch. That would make

me so happy if you just took me to lunch." And he would lis-
ten to it, and he would never do it. Never, ever would do it.

Besides failing to respond when their partners ask for more connection and quality time, abusers also refuse to show care and concern when it is warranted:

> *He had a car and could've just picked me up from work, but*
> *he didn't. I remember one day spending two hours trying to*
> *get home on the bus. It didn't come, and I had to walk a long*
> *time and figure out how to go. It was nine o'clock at night*
> *when I finally got home, and he was playing video games. I*
> *said, "Oh, my gosh, it took me so long to get here." And he*
> *said, "Well, yeah. That's what buses are like." And he kept*
> *playing the video game. I couldn't believe it.*
>
> —Paige

It is a truism of human relationships that joys shared are multiplied, and sorrows shared are minimized. That is equally true about the small frustrations, fears, and hurts of daily life as well as the big events. Abused people are regularly denied the benefits of sharing life's emotions with their partners because abusers consistently fail to connect with them in a loving, empathic way.

MANIPULATION VIOLATES
RELATIONSHIP TRUST

Another especially egregious betrayal of trust is when abusers use gaslighting and other forms of manipulation on their partner, because they are actually using the partner's fundamental relationship trust as a tool to mislead and harm them:

*I believed he loved me, so why would he lie? Why would he
say something that wasn't true? He's smart and he loves me.
This is my husband, so I need to listen to what he is saying.
What is wrong with me?*

—SAMANTHA

The belief that their significant other is an emotionally safe person makes partners an easy target for the abuser.

Becca shared the devastating effect her ex's gaslighting had on her even after she was with a loving partner:

*He would make things up that people said about me that
weren't true. He would tell me horrible things about me, and
about my body, that it was disgusting. I got to the point that
I started believing the things he was telling me.*

*I was very self-conscious because of things that my ex had said
about my body. And my new husband is so good about reassuring me that he thinks I am beautiful and there is nothing wrong with me. He would never put me down or talk to
me like my ex did, ever. It is completely different. Completely.
Even though my husband has done an amazing job of making me feel beautiful, I think I still carry those things in the
back of my mind sometimes—being self-conscious when I
am intimate with him.*

Ironically, trust is essential to both healthy partnerships and emotional abuse. Emotional abuse derives a lot of its power from the misplaced belief that the abuser is an emotionally trustworthy person with their partner's best interests at heart. Tragically, in the hands of abusers, that trust is used to devalue, demean, and manipulate, striking at the very essence of their partner's being.

THE ABUSER'S EVER-CHANGING CONTRACT

One way abusers gain and keep power in a partnership is through their ever-changing relationship contract. The abuser's Dr. Jekyll/Mr. Hyde pattern of behavior that randomly mixes loving acts with abusiveness is actually part of the abuse process. It takes advantage of the partner's trust to enhance the abuser's power-over position and disempower the abused partner.

THE TOXIC MIX OF LOVE AND ABUSE

The abuser's loving behavior draws partners in at the beginning of a relationship. It reassures them and keeps them holding onto hope during the relationship. And it lures them back when they start to pull away or take steps to end the relationship:

> *The hardest part was coming to the realization that no matter what I did, no matter how hard I tried, he was never going to be the person I knew that first year. And that was what kept me for so long. I was thinking he is going to be awesome like that again.*
>
> —BECCA

Abusive behaviors shock and disorient. They erode the partner's self-esteem, self-image, and self-confidence, and lead to depression and despair:

> *I was stunned. I felt like I entered a strange land, and I didn't know how to navigate. Nothing made sense. The person who loved me so much that he couldn't live without me suddenly started treating me so badly. He was so mean.*
>
> —TERRI

*I started completely losing my sense of self. I just kind of with-
ered away with the chronic stress and the constant hateful-
ness. I felt myself dying inside.*

—SABRINA

The unpredictable alternation between loving and abusive behaviors repeatedly pulls partners from hurt to hope and back again. It
keeps them preoccupied trying to figure out what went wrong and
how to fix it, and leads to confusion, frustration, and disempowerment:

*She was predictably unpredictable. I never knew what was
going to set her off. That was the most harmful part of it
because I never knew what she was going to be like when I
walked in the door.*

—PETE

All of the above keeps the power imbalance in the relationship
skewed in favor of the abuser. Never knowing why or when their
significant other will change from kind to cruel puts a person in an
ongoing state of anxiety that is emotionally, mentally, and physically
exhausting. When they are so diminished and depleted that the abuser's acts of kindness feel like a welcome relief, or even a generous gift,
abused partners can become increasingly attached to the abuser. That
attachment forms a traumatic bond that makes it difficult for people to break away from abusive relationships.[8]

THE LURE

Of course, at the beginning of a relationship, most people put
their best foot forward, including future abusers. Abusers usually
present a very different face to the outside world than they do to
their intimate partners. So in the beginning, potential partners, like

other people in the abuser's life, believe in the public image of the future abuser:

> *He was such a great guy ... well-liked ... thoughtful ... charming ... caring.*
>
> *Everybody loved her.... never heard a bad word ... lots of friends ... kind ... sweet ... funny.*
>
> —CQ

It is easy for someone to get drawn in by the flush of strong feelings and all the promise that a new love relationship holds. What's more, the excitement and attraction of the dating period can lead people to overlook or minimize any possible red flags that do show up. Furthermore, if their family of origin was abusive, they may not recognize danger signs at all.

THE SWITCH

In addition to what common wisdom teaches us about relationships, people also have shared ideas of what romantic behavior is supposed to look like based on love stories, songs, poems, and movies. So abusers know how to act to attract a partner. A familiar story for many abused people is that their partner showed them a very appealing side before there was a commitment. Once an intimate partnership was formed, the abuser began to shift from the promise of a loving relationship to the power-over relationship of abuse. Eaglin and Matt's relationship provides a helpful example:

> *In the beginning, he was incredibly complimentary and put me on a pedestal.*
>
> *He was silly, he was a great storyteller, he was incredibly*

brilliant, and he was able to talk about social justice, and communicate as if he held so much empathy, and he presented himself as humble. I really believed the fantasy. The good is that he saves the world and holds values that are important to me.

Matt's dating behavior indicated that empathy was a primary value for him, and it was a quality that attracted Eaglin. Based on his pre-commitment attitudes, she thought that they had shared values and were forming a relationship contract based on empathy. But shortly after their marriage, Matt began ridiculing, criticizing, shaming, ignoring, and threatening her. He coerced her into doing what he wanted and terrorized her with anger when she didn't comply with his wishes. He even coached their young children to treat their mother with disdain.

Eaglin became so overwhelmed, disoriented, and beaten down by the abuse that it wasn't until Matt told her she didn't deserve to live that she finally got the help she needed and found the inner strength to leave. Far from the relationship contract based on the empathy she saw in their pre-commitment partnership, she got one nearly devoid of human kindness.

Even when abusive situations are more subtle, they are still disconcerting, disorienting, and destructive to abused partners. The undercover nature of the abuse keeps people unsure of what is going on, and the positive times keep them hoping for something better:

As soon as we were married, something changed. The sex was good. Being together was good. But he started not valuing me or my decisions. I wanted it to change and be more fair, but I thought I just needed to try harder to make it work. I kept thinking it would get better. He would realize that it wasn't fair, and his behavior would change.

—Marjorie

In the beginning, it can be hard to tell the difference between the typical adjustments of learning to live together and the first steps of emotional abuse. The hurtful times can seem like mistakes or misunderstandings in an otherwise loving relationship.

THE HOPE

Abused partners are often so convinced that the characteristics that first attracted them to the abuser are the "true" person, that they make allowances for abusive actions because they think they are out of character, and something else must be causing the hurtful behavior. The abuser's recurring, albeit inconsistent, positive interactions with them reinforce that idea:

> *He was a very nice person. As crazy as that sounds, he was very cool and nice to people. I would minimize it because sometimes he would be so wonderful. He was so good to me and so loving that I would just brush off the bad times in hopes that he would stop treating me that way.*
>
> *I had rose-colored glasses. I knew how kind he could be, so I would forgive him for being so mean because I believed that wasn't who he really was, but it actually was who he really was.*
>
> —BECCA

Partners stay hoping things will get back to "normal," and during the positive times it looks like they do. But abuse gradually becomes the new norm.

Abused people are not alone in misreading the abuser. Partners often lose their support systems when others don't believe their complaints because of the abuser's Dr. Jekyll/Mr. Hyde style:

Nobody believed me. I told four friends. Every one of them said, "Really? You've got him and this is what you're saying? I would kill to have him as my boyfriend. He would never act like that. Why are you doing this to him?" They all turned their backs on me. I didn't have anywhere to go because none of my friends believed me, at least for a period of time.

—WARREN

When abused partners can't connect with a validating person and don't have the benefit of a reality check from someone outside the relationship, they become less sure of themselves, more vulnerable to the abuse, and more likely to be lulled back into a false sense of security by the good times.

THE PULL BACK

Just as abusers promise a loving partnership to lure their partners in at the beginning of the relationship, and intermittently offer kindness in the midst of the abuse to keep their partners hanging on to hope during the relationship, they will hold out a better relationship contract when it looks like the partner is ready to end it:

The handful of times when I would leave, the things she would say to get me back were exactly the things I wanted to believe, and I wanted her to be. One reason I stayed so long was because I truly believed that the woman I thought I met in the beginning was a good person.

—ELLEN

When people struggle with leaving an emotionally abusive relationship, they frequently come back to the idea that their partner has good qualities that make the relationship worth saving.

TRAUMATIC BONDING

The danger of the abuser's unpredictable shifts between loving and abusive behavior goes beyond the constant rekindling of hope, though. People are especially in need of comfort and care when they are distressed. But in emotional abuse, the person causing the distress and the person giving the comfort are usually the same:

> *When he would yell at me, it just shut me down, and then I'd get panicky and have anxiety, and then eventually he would try to comfort me. He was comforting me for something that he did, but I was like "Oh, affection, attention. Yay, he does love me!"*
>
> —CHLOE

The abuser's combination of loving acts and mistreatment often lead the partner to become even more attached to the abuser, always hoping for another sign that they are loved and valued by their significant other.[9]

Sabrina explains how she felt both safe and unsafe with her husband. Although she experienced extreme emotional abuse in the relationship, when she describes his kindnesses, the abuse seems to fade into the background of her story:

> *He wanted me to feel special. He thought I was special. When he was calm and nothing was bothering him and I wasn't bothering him, then he would be very patient with me. And when he took care of me when I was sick—I felt so unsafe with his behaviors, but he was also the person who made me feel the safest because he would protect me and take good care of me. When I wasn't irritating him, he was extremely nurturing. When he was a good guy, he was a really good guy.*

She was only safe as long he was calm and nothing was bothering him, but it was the caretaking that stood out in her experience. Sabrina goes on to explain how much the positives meant to her:

> *We don't stay because of the abuse. We stay because of something else that seems to make up for the abuse, that seems to be so beautiful or magical that it makes the relationship worth saving. That was true for me.*

Facing hostility and/or rejection from a beloved partner raises stress hormones in a person's body. And experiencing a loving, empathic connection releases "feel-good" hormones.[10] So when the random loving acts release a flood of feel-good hormones in a body that is regularly saturated with stress hormones, the feel-good sensation can act like an addictive substance:[11]

> *I compared it to a heroin addict. I felt like I was going through withdrawals from him. I wouldn't talk to him because I was afraid he would talk me into coming back, and I was trying to stay away from the drug.*
>
> —ALICE

The abuser's manipulation of relationship trust helps to explain how people get drawn into abusive partnerships, why they stay, and what makes it so hard to leave.

SUMMARY

Relationship Trust

- People have a basic human need to feel safe, valued, and cared for by a trusted loved one.

- That trust makes people vulnerable to each other.

- Abusers regularly violate relationship trust by actively devaluing their partners, refusing to make a loving connection with them, or taking advantage of their trust to manipulate them.

The Abuser's Ever-Changing Contract

- The abuser's shift from loving to abusive behavior is part of the abuse process.

- The loving times keep the partner hoping for a better relationship and focused on doing what it takes to make the relationship a success.

- The combination can lead to traumatic bonding: a kind of attachment that makes it hard for people to separate from the abuser.

ACTIVITY

1. Can you trust your partner to be there for you when you are vulnerable, or when you have a need?

2. Do you feel emotionally as well as physically safe in your relationship? If not, what happens that makes you feel unsafe?

3. Overall, do you feel valued by your partner? If not, what happens to make you feel devalued?

4. Are there ways in which your partner used your trust in them to harm or manipulate you? How?

5. Has your partner used your confidences or vulnerabilities against you, or ever threatened to do so? How?

6. For one month, keep a private calendar or journal to note your partner's swings between loving and hurtful behaviors. In a few words, note how you feel after the hurtful times, then how you feel after the loving behavior.

7. Are you frequently unsure of where you stand with your partner? What affect does that have on you?

8. Is your relationship a major source of stress in your life? In what ways?

IS IT SUPPOSED TO BE THIS HARD?

No. Healthy partners can count on each other to be there for them when they have a need or are vulnerable. Through their actions and words, they show that they appreciate and value each other.

Unexplained Dr. Jekyll/Mr. Hyde type behaviors are not part of a healthy relationship. Although moods fluctuate and couples get upset with each other sometimes, their level of respect, care and consideration is generally consistent. Healthy couples are kind to each other the vast majority of the time.

CHAPTER 4

UNSPOKEN CONTRACTS AND THE FAMILY OF ORIGIN

"I Thought It Was Just Part of Being Married"

My mother and father were emotionally abusive. That's why I didn't recognize it, because I grew up with it. I grew up thinking it was my fault. I had no clue they were abusive until I got into therapy. I had no clue my husband was, either. It's true that he was being unfair and mean, but I felt like I deserved it, because that's my history. My parents were that way. I wrote it off as, "That is what relationships are."

—JACKIE

Although not all abused partners come from abusive families, most do.[12] If you witnessed abuse between your parents, you likely developed ideas about how adult partnerships work based on what you saw, ideas that made you vulnerable to abuse in your own adult relationships. And if one or both of your parents were abusive toward you, you likely learned to accept poor treatment from a loved one. In addition, if you are like Jackie and didn't realize that what happened to you as a child was abuse, it would make sense that when the same kinds of things happened with your partner, you wouldn't know they were abusive, either.

What children from abusive families learn about relationships ultimately lays the groundwork for the unconscious and unequal relationship contract that forms the basis for abusive partnerships. But children who grow up to become abusers and those who later become abused partners take very different lessons about relationships from their families.

For children, the family household is their world. When they see abuse happening, they surmise that this is just the way things are:

> *That last day he was screaming and throwing things, so I went in to get my daughter and said, "Come on, we're leaving," and she said, "What? Why? I don't want to leave Dad."️ That was another wake-up call for me, "Oh, man, she thinks this is normal."*

> —Anika

When conflict, tension, anxiety, and fear are part of a person's ongoing reality from early in life, they don't know that things can and should be different. So, they more readily accept or perpetuate those behaviors.

THE PARENTS' RELATIONSHIP

One important influence on a child's understanding of love relationships is how they see the adults in their life treat each other. The parents' relationship stands as an example of what partnerships are supposed to be:

> *They constantly bickered, argued, fought, and sometimes physically fought. So, I thought if you love someone, you just have*

to put up with them no matter what, because that's what
love is. No matter what they do, you just have to deal with
it. That was what I saw. Then my mom was the one that
was begging for love, so I thought that was something I was
supposed to do, also. And my mom had the belief that the
woman should be taken care of and shouldn't have to work.
So, I thought it was OK to sort of live under someone.

—CHLOE

Parents are our first role models. It is from them that people learn how to act in adult relationships. In traditional hetero families, boys learn how to be men and interact with women by watching the father figure in the family, and girls learn how to be women and interact with men from watching the mother figure.

Even when a person pointedly decides not to be like an abusive or abused parent, the rejection of that model still influences their adult behavior. Children with LGBTQ+ parents may not have the same gender associations, but no doubt, any abuse between parent figures will leave a lasting imprint on a child and influence their adult partnerships.

THE PARENT-CHILD RELATIONSHIP

Another important factor that influences children's developing idea of relationship contracts is how they are treated by each parent figure. Pete never saw his parents in conflict but was emotionally abused by his mother. The combination left him unprepared to effectively respond to his wife's abuse:

It started as soon as we got back from the honeymoon—
the put-downs, the blaming, the raging. My parents had
a great relationship and always treated each other with

respect. I never saw them fight. I never even heard them
have a loud argument, so I was shocked at the way my wife
started treating me. It felt like I entered some kind of dysto-
pia. I had no idea adults treated each other that way, and
I didn't know how to respond to her. But my mom, she was
a rager. She was hyper-critical, controlling, and judgmen-
tal, so when my wife started that kind of stuff, I did what
I always did: tried to figure out how to fix things so she
wouldn't get so upset. When that didn't work, I just tried
to stay out of her way.

A person's primary caretaker is their first love relationship. What
they learn there will carry forward to their future partnerships.

HOW CHILDREN LEARN TO COPE

There have been volumes written about how family of origin
experiences shape adult behavior. The subject is so complex that no
single book covers every aspect of the topic. But simply put, children who are likely to become abusers have learned that the only
way to be safe in relationship is to have power and control over their
important others. And children who are likely to become abused
partners have learned that the surest way to be safe in relationship
is to notice and respond to the needs and demands of others before
things become scary.[13]

For instance, some children who feel terrorized by a raging parent may manage their fear by deciding that the safest thing to do is
become as strong and forceful as the abuser. Their belief is, "It is dan-
gerous to be weak. I can never let them know I'm scared. I can never
let them know I hurt. I must become as strong or stronger than the
abuser. If I am powerful enough, I will be safe." Pete appeared to be
on the receiving end of that kind of thinking:

> *It was like she decided I was her enemy. I know her dad*
> *was an alcoholic who was abusive to the kids. It was like*
> *my wife decided the best defense was a good offense. I guess*
> *she couldn't get back at her dad, so she took it out on me*
> *instead. She was always ready to take offense and be angry*
> *at me over one thing or the other. I couldn't do anything*
> *right in her eyes.*

Other children may look at a raging parent and conclude that the best way to protect themselves is to be aware of the abuser's moods and take care of anything that might set them off. Their thinking goes, "If I can fix things, be good enough, make everything better, make them feel better, then I will be safe." Marjorie explains the effect her father's violence had on her:

> *My father would come home after a night of drinking and*
> *decide the house wasn't clean enough. He would wake us all*
> *up in the middle of the night, screaming and yelling and*
> *make us start cleaning. I started anticipating what would*
> *get him going so I could take care of it before he got violent.*
> *Even after I grew up and got a job I kept doing that. I was*
> *a great employee because I was always on the lookout for*
> *what needed to be done and did it before anyone asked or*
> *even noticed.*

Abused children instinctively know that their survival depends on the very person who frightens, harms, or neglects them. *So their reactions are not just coping mechanisms, they are survival strategies.* When this is learned before a person can speak or reason, it becomes part of their identity and drives their adult behavior. If two people with such different ideas of how relationships work become partners, an abusive situation is almost inevitable.

BRINGING IT FORWARD

A power imbalance is the central issue in abusive partnerships. Whether the couple realizes it or not, most of their problems are related to the abuser's need for power and control. The partner's efforts to solve those problems don't work because *the abuser's behavior is still unconsciously driven by the terrified child within who believes to the core of their being that having dominance in an intimate relationship is a survival issue.* Anything they perceive as a challenge will trigger that fear and elicit defensive and offensive reactions that translate into abuse. And abusers often feel challenged when their partners do what most healthy adults do, such as assert their individuality; express their own ideas, preferences, or needs; disagree with the abuser; or object to mistreatment:

> *Me being too independent was a problem. I had my own life, my own career, a lot of community. It was my fault for being too independent.*
>
> —ABIGAIL

> *If I was doing things he didn't want me to do, like going to the store without him or calling one of my friends to go do something, if I didn't do those things, we wouldn't have these problems.*
>
> —BECCA

If abused partners manage to stop or sidestep the abuse one way, the abuser is compelled to assert power another way, so emotional abuse seems to have endless variations. *Abusers simply don't feel safe unless they believe that they are firmly in control of their partner and the relationship.*

WHY COMPASSION DOESN'T WORK

Since the abuser's family experiences taught them that they must have power and control to be safe, they often come to detest the weakness that made them vulnerable as a child, so they resolve to avoid vulnerability at all costs. Meanwhile, abused partners, whose childhood experiences taught them to tend to the needs of others, hope to heal the abuser with love and compassion. But receiving compassion requires a certain kind of vulnerability, so the partner's attempts at being a source of compassionate healing usually backfire:

> *I always had a feeling that there was something going on with her under the surface. And I wanted to go there. I wanted to understand what the superficial stuff was about. So I would try to get more intimate, more understanding, and she would completely discount it. She was completely disinterested in any type of emotional vulnerability, connection, anything like that.*
>
> —ELLEN

Instead of providing relief, offers of compassion remind the abuser of the detested childhood weakness that must be denied and rejected. Consequently, the partner's efforts to understand and heal are ignored, taken advantage of, or twisted in a way that allows the abuser to maintain their sense of strength and dominance.

Paola, who was emotionally abused in multiple relationships, shares some hard-won wisdom:

> *I believed in my healing capability. My unconditional love was going to heal them and their primary wounds. Not taking into account that certain personalities can never get past the wounding of family of origin. What I've noticed is the abuser's depth of insecurity, and how their ego will try to quash my ego.*

In addition to despising their own vulnerability, some abusers also despise vulnerability in others. Such people see their partner's compassion and consideration as a weakness that deserves contempt rather than as a loving gift. Instead of receiving the hoped-for healing, abusers are triggered to increase the abuse. In order to protect their own wounded ego, they are willing to quash their partner's ego.

A SENSE OF ENTITLEMENT

Besides abuse, there is another style of parenting that can lead children to become abusive adults: overindulgence. Children who are constantly catered to and not held accountable for problem behaviors are likely to develop a sense of entitlement, expecting others to give in to their whims and adjust to their way of doing things. That attitude can become so deeply ingrained that when they don't get their way, they see it, not just as a disappointment, but as a provocation or injustice that deserves retaliation:

> *If I would leave and not come back when he told me to come back, he would throw away all my pictures or my Bible, something he knew was important to me. He would get rid of them to punish me.*
>
> —BECCA

Abusers tend to see their maltreatment of their partners as a justifiable rebalancing of the scales that returns them to a position of power and control, which in their view is the way things should be.

In heterosexual relationships, the attitudes and habits of male privilege feed into and reinforce a male abuser's treatment of his female partner. However, an outsized sense of entitlement is a hallmark of any abuser regardless of the gender combination in their partnerships. Their relationship contract goes something like, "I am special and must be treated as special at all times. Because you are not nearly as special as I am, your needs and wants don't matter. If you complain about my behavior, challenge me in any way, or fail to treat me as the special person I am, you have harmed me grievously and deserve to be punished." Here is an example:

> *If I tried to initiate a discussion about something I thought was wrong, she would get angry and say I was ruining everything. A simple argument about something small would result in her pulling her rings off her hand, throwing them at me, and screaming at me about divorce. This could be an argument about cleaning the kitchen sink, or the oven, or not putting laundry away.*
>
> —Vincent

Regardless of whether it comes from childhood overindulgence or the idea that they have a right to harm others to protect their own ego, a sense of entitlement is a key part of an abuser's personality.

Another reason why it can be hard for abused partners to tell the difference between emotional abuse and the hard work of relationships is that they usually don't recognize abuse because it was part of the environment they grew up in. When children live with abuse they learn to adapt to abusive treatment:

> *The key to understanding what is going on is seeing how your childhood prepared you to accept abuse as an adult. My issues originated long before I met my abusive partner and allowed him to disrespect me.*
>
> —CQ

The good news is that what was learned can be unlearned, and new, healthier ways of relating can become the new normal instead.

ADDITIONAL CONSIDERATIONS

While the above descriptions explain a lot of what lies behind emotional abuse, they are not comprehensive. For example, sibling abuse can be a precursor to abuse in adult relationships. In addition, parental abandonment often leads to the extreme jealousy, isolating, and stalking behaviors of some abusers. It can also put abused partners at risk of accepting abuse out of fear of being abandoned by their loved one.

It is also important to note that most people who were raised in abusive households do not go on to become abusers. In addition, there are people who do not describe abusive families of origin who become abused partners. And there are people who were raised in a loving and healthy manner, without abuse, whose negative behaviors alarm and mystify their own parents. This can be due to chemical imbalances or other mental health issues.

For more information on how families of origin affect abused partners, see "Understanding the Family of Origin and Abuse" on pages 222-225.

SUMMARY

- People learn from their family of origin about how to act in relationships, and what kinds of actions from others are acceptable. How their parents treated each other, and how each parent treated them as a child influences their future relationships.

- Children who grow up to be abusers have learned that having power and control over their partner is the only way to be safe in relationship, and/or they were overindulged and raised with so few boundaries that they developed no sense of accountability or empathy.

- Abused partners learned that the best way to stay safe in relationships is to focus on and tend to the needs of others.

ACTIVITY

1. How did your parents treat each other in your family of origin? Has that affected the way you interact with your current partner? How?

2. Are there similarities in how one or both of your parents treated you and the way your partner treats you? If so, what are they?

3. Do you regularly feel compelled to tend to others' needs at the expense of your own? How has that played out in your relationship?

4. Does it seem to you that your partner needs to have power and control in the relationship? In what ways?

IS IT SUPPOSED TO BE THIS HARD?

No. Few people escape childhood without wounds to their psyche. But most people learn ways to heal and manage those wounds in ways that don't cause ongoing harm to others. Healthy people balance their own needs with those of their partners.

CHAPTER 5

SUBTLETY PART I
"But It's Not That Bad"

I thought all relationships have their problems. Since he never hit me, I didn't recognize it as abuse. I just knew that he was very angry and very hurtful.

—SIERRA

I experienced a lot of confusion, a lot of unhappiness and discontent with the relationship, but I couldn't understand why that was. I didn't know exactly what was going on that caused that kind of void.

—ELLEN

If you are like Sierra, it may seem that although you are unhappy in your relationship, and your partner is sometimes—or often—hurtful and inconsiderate, it doesn't rise to the level of abuse. Or, like Ellen, you may have a sense that there is something wrong, but you can't quite put your finger on it. The problems in the relationship don't seem to explain the level of hurt, anxiety, sadness, and resentment that you often feel.

That is because subtle emotional abuse happens in an ongoing series of minor everyday events that gradually accumulate over time.

It blends in with the ordinary activities of daily life, making it hard for a person living in the middle of it to see it or explain it to themselves, let alone anyone else. Emotionally abused partners usually feel the abuse long before they see it.

This subtle abuse is hidden in attitudes and overriding assumptions that create the atmosphere the couple lives in. It shows up in facial expressions and other non-verbals like sighs, head shakes, shrugs, or simply not acknowledging you at all. It's in the way conversations happen, and how they end. It's also in the gradual building up of thoughtless, unkind, and hurtful actions that are so small they seem insignificant at the time. These daily interactions shape another aspect of the unconscious and unequal relationship contract that is the foundation of emotional abuse.

IT'S IN THE ATTITUDE

Emotional abusers are not usually stereotypical villains. They have positive qualities that their partners love, things that attracted them in the first place, and many couples do have some good times together. However, abusers also have an attitude of entitlement, the idea that they are superior and should be favored over others, and things should go their way, no questions asked. That attitude of privilege is constantly in the background, but often goes unnoticed. All the while it quietly sets up an unequal distribution of power.

In an emotionally abusive relationship, this attitude can be so pervasive and so subtle that it is easy for the other person to get swept along with it while being unaware of what is happening, as the following story describes:

> *Two things started happening, I think, soon after we were married. I don't even remember how it started. One is that*

if I was standing nearby when he was doing something, he would hand me trash, like a pull-off strip from packaging, or an empty envelope, and I would take it from him and throw it away. I don't know if I thought I was being courteous, or helpful, or if it was just a reflex, but I somehow fed into his assumption that I would be there to take care of his discards. What is amazing is that it took me years to realize what was happening. I know I felt annoyed by it before I actually got what was going on. When I finally stopped doing it, he got irritated with me—disgruntled, like I was being unreasonable by not tending to his trash.

It took me even longer to see the other thing. When I had something to say to him, I would go to the room where he was and say it. When he had something to say to me, he would call out for me to come to wherever he was. It didn't make any difference what I was doing or where I was in the house. His expectation was that I should stop whatever it was I was doing and go see what he wanted. Again, I don't know how I got pulled into that assumption, either, except it seems like when you are living with someone, and they call out to you, you go see what they want. Don't normal people do that? Anyway, it's what I did for years until I noticed it was all one way. Like the trash thing, I felt irritated before I knew what I was irritated about. There were even times when he would call out with a sense of urgency, like something terrible happened that needed my attention right away. I would drop what I was doing and rush over. When I got there, he'd ask me some mundane question that could have easily waited for a casual conversation, like: Where do you want to go for vacation? I think it was those times that helped me see what was going on.

—TERRI

Similarly, another person described how her partner would never answer the door or phone, nor would he get up to let the dog in or out. She just took care of those things without thinking about it because they needed to be done. She, too, took a long time to realize that her partner's attitude was that it was her job to handle those things, and he had no intention of being bothered with them. In their entitled approach to the relationship, these abusers subtly cast their partners as servants.

Going to a partner who calls from another room, taking discards when one person has their hands full, or one person doing more pet tending than the other are the sorts of things that happen in most relationships. Any one of these things happening occasionally, or by mutual agreement, is not abusive. But when they are ongoing and part of a larger pattern of disrespect, disregard, and devaluing, they add to the abusive picture. They are like the background colors in a thousand-piece jigsaw puzzle, not adding anything obvious to the picture itself, but a pervasive presence all the same.

IT'S IN THE DECISION MAKING

Another way abusers show an attitude of entitlement is in how they make unilateral decisions in the relationship. Abusers consistently take control of deciding things large and small, from how the money is spent to what movies or TV shows they will watch, regularly dismissing or ignoring their partner's ideas and preferences. At first glance, these issues may look like simple disagreements that need to be worked out. And the partners may perceive them that way, at least in the beginning. But abusers are not really proposing an idea to be discussed. They are asserting how things will be:

We bought a 75-year-old home before the kids were born.
Shortly after buying, it he told me that the inside was mine

to fix and the outdoor work was his (mowing the lawn and fixing the car). He refused to help inside, but even when it came time to paint the outside, he was nowhere to be found.

—MARJORIE

This abuser enforced his will by ignoring his partner's objections and refusing her requests for help.

Sometimes partners are shut out of the decision-making process when the abuser just does what they want without consulting the other person or considering how it affects them. Alec explains:

She referred to my work time as my adult time. My kid time was when I come home. Her kid time was during the day, so her adult time had to be in the evening, "You know that the evenings belong to me. I'm going out." It turned into almost every day, though. Then the tasks start piling up. I'd come home and she hadn't done anything the whole day. Hadn't prepared a meal or washed their clothes, so now it's not just taking care of them, it is doing everything that was supposed to be done during the day. Those things tell you who dictates the schedule, who says how things go.

—ALEC

In abusive relationships, there is often no discussion, no debate, no deciding together. The abuser just goes forward with their plans. In mutually respectful relationships, there is reciprocity. Decisions are made collaboratively after talking things through and making compromises.

A times the abuser's control of decisions is hard to discern because it blends in with the good parts of the relationship:

I was an art student, creative, sensitive, athletic but not out-doorsy. We went to sporting events instead of art museums.

We mountain hiked, sailed, downhill skied, canoed, camped in isolated areas where he could fish. When we had kids and camped, I took care of the kids while he fished. In retrospect, I enjoyed learning those things, but there was no balance or opportunity for me to decide where we would vacation. We never visited my friends. Our summer vacations consisted of going to his best friend's place on the East Coast and sailing. Hard to complain, I know, but year after year I never visited my friends or got to choose where I wanted to go.

—Marjorie

The abuser's attitude shows that their thoughts and plans are the only ones that matter to them. Regularly making choices for another adult without their input or consent is an inherently abusive act. It doesn't really matter how big or small the issue may be; the real issue is that one person is making a power play that disempowers the other.

IT'S IN THE LOOKS

Consistent disapproving, condescending, or threatening looks are part of the emotional abuse picture. Rolling the eyes, glaring, scowling, smirking, a furrowed brow, and slight shaking of the head are just some of the ways abusers use looks to express disdain toward their partners. These expressions can last just seconds and, though not a word has been spoken, a negative message has been sent.

Humans see themselves through the eyes of the people who are important to them. The reflections they observe in the faces of their loved ones have a powerful impact on their self-perception. When a person sees significantly more positive than negative reflections, they feel a sense of acceptance and security, while regular negative reflections sow self-doubt and severely undermine a person's sense of belonging and emotional safety. In the following example, an abuser literally gives a negative reflection to his partner:

> *One day early in our marriage, I had just gotten out of the shower and was in front of the mirror putting on moisturizer. My husband came in the bathroom and noticed I still had water droplets between my shoulder blades and down my back. In what I thought was going to be a moment of sweet intimacy, he took a towel and dried off my back, but then he looked at my reflection in the mirror, frowned, shook his head, and looked at me like I was a hopeless idiot. Then he hung up the towel and, left the room. I can't even tell you how I felt—hurt, but more than that, deflated, lonely, a sinking feeling. The rest of the day went on like nothing happened. I didn't forget it; it still hurt, but it kind of got glossed over.*

—TERRI

Many emotionally abusive events are both fleeting and disorienting. Often, before someone can begin to process what has just occurred, the busyness of the day takes over. Maybe there is a rush to get to work, the kids need something, the phone rings, or a meal needs tending. Sometimes abused partners don't know why they feel bad, they just know they do. Unspoken messages are insidious because there is nothing tangible to debate, discuss, defend, or argue against.

IT'S IN THE CONVERSATIONS

Much to the partner's frustration and confusion, emotional abusers are masters at not communicating. They avoid conversations in a variety of ways when their partners have complaints, for instance saying, "I don't want to talk about that now," walking away, using anger to intimidate their partner, or twisting things around to blame them.

But many abusers will also sabotage communication even when there is no complaint or conflict involved, making regular, everyday conversations difficult. One way they do that is by ignoring their partners or giving them minimal responses that show a casual disinterest in what they are saying:

> *I could look at him and see that he started tuning me out almost as soon as I started talking.*
>
> *He would start ignoring me in the middle of a conversation. There were times I stopped talking mid-sentence and he never seemed to notice. Here's an example. We were at a restaurant, and I was talking about our vacation plans. Then he started watching a video that someone at the next table had on their iPad. I stopped talking and he didn't notice. When he finally brought his attention back to the table, he didn't even acknowledge that he'd gotten distracted, or that I had been talking. He started off on another topic. That kind of thing happen over and over, but when I confronted him about it, he acted like I was picking on him, and the conversation went nowhere.*
>
> —TERRI

Though they were in the middle of a pleasant outing, the abuser slipped in a message of disregard for his partner, then went back to a casual conversation as if nothing happened. Subtle emotional abuse shows up unexpectedly, sometimes amid what would otherwise be an enjoyable time. In a relationship where things go well part of the time, these casually abusive events are a disheartening and demeaning surprise.

Even when abusers engage in a discussion, they often refuse to acknowledge their partner's side of the conversation. Abusers will emphatically repeat their own points while ignoring what their partner has to say, bring up a different topic, or answer with something totally irrelevant:

> *Our conversations often go off the rails. She will take a statement I made and create a statement that is different in some insidious way and start responding to that. For a second it looks and sounds like we're talking about the same thing, but we're not. Then I have no idea where we are or what we are talking about. I am completely confused. The character of the whole thing has just changed, and I'm lost.*
>
> —VINCENT

Conversations with abusers often go through twists and turns that baffle, frustrate, and discourage their partner.

Another way abusers twist conversations is when they create a seemingly purposeful misunderstanding of what the partner said:

> *She will take whatever I said and blow it out to extremes.*
>
> —VINCENT

> *I just finished reading a book and set down on the coffee table and said, "Wow, that was a great book. You should read it." And she said, "Don't tell me what to do! You wouldn't talk to your friends that way!" I was stunned and confused. I talk to my friends that way all the time, and no one else acts like recommending a book is the same thing as bossing them around.*
>
> —PETE

Never knowing what to expect is something abused partners live with. For instance, conversations go well often enough that they feel shocked and wounded when the abuser unexpectedly responds with irritation, hostility, or indifference.

Abusers express undercover hostility in daily conversations many ways. One way is to mask their debasement of their partners behind a thin veil of caring:

> *I would be trying to have a serious conversation and my husband would look at me with the kind of amused look someone would have when listening to a precocious child, like he was trying hard not to break out laughing. When I confronted him about it, he told me how cute and endearing I was. Then he got offended because I objected to being treated like a child. Other people respect my intelligence, but my husband treated me like a child a lot.*
>
> —TERRI

Another way is by making a habit of negating them:

> *I would make a statement, then he would say, "No, that's wrong," and then basically repeat what I just said. Sometimes he would talk like he was explaining a complicated subject I would have difficulty understanding.*
>
> —TERRI

Sometimes they correct their partners unnecessarily:

> *One night we went for a walk on the beach. I was so excited to see one of those big harvest moons close to the horizon. I said, "Oh, look, a full moon." He took an irritated tone and said, "That's not a full moon. It won't be full until tomorrow."*
>
> —TERRI

In addition to arguing minor points and irrelevancies, abusers also do things like discredit their partner in front of others, even when they are not wrong. Sometimes they won't let a topic go until the partner agrees that the abuser is right. Some abusers don't just need to be right; they need their partner to be wrong. In order to feel superior, they cast their partner as inferior.

Often it is not what is said, but how it is said that expresses disdain:

> *I didn't ever understand where the irritated tone of voice came from. He used an ugly tone of voice so often I finally asked him what would happen if he talked to people at work the way he talked to me. He said, "I would get fired." But that admission didn't open his eyes at all. He kept on doing it.*
>
> —Terri

In loving relationships, conversations are a way for couples to connect. In emotionally abusive relationships, they often become another way in which partners experience a sense of rejection, hurt, and loss.

IT'S IN THE SMALL STUFF

Subtle abuse also shows up in small things that are part of everyday interactions. Although these things seem trivial, and hardly worth mentioning when talking about abuse, they accumulate over time and communicate an attitude of disregard and disrespect that devalues the abused person. One way abusers devalue their partners is through constant criticism. "I couldn't do anything right," is a typical comment abused people make.

But in addition to being openly critical, abusers also use indirect methods that are harder to detect:

> *He had been waiting for me in the car at a craft store. When*

I came out, he mentioned how all the women who went in were fat. He hated fat people and was an athlete with no body issues. I struggled with my weight. Another time he was waiting in the car at my college, and he said all the students looked like nerds. Those comments were painful, but at that time I couldn't put my finger on why they made me feel bad.

—MARJORIE

Name-calling can also be done indirectly:

If I made little mistakes like pulling on a "push" door, or thinking it was Wednesday when it was really Tuesday, he would shake his head and say, "Stupid" under his breath. He was always mumbling about me being stupid.

—TERRI

Although they seem to be petty, a regular diet of those sideways criticisms and put-downs, especially from a loved one, negatively affects a person's self-perception and confidence.

Abusers also use blaming and shaming to denigrate their partners. Small mishaps are a part of life and occur fairly regularly. When an abuser's style is to place blame for those things, their partner becomes an easy and constant target:

We made a grocery list and then got ready to go to the store. We both walked out and left the list on the kitchen table. All the way back home I had to hear about how irresponsible I was. Either one of us could have picked up the list, neither one of us did, but somehow it was my fault and she needed to make sure I knew it.

—PETE

When the original blinds in a fifty-year-old house fell apart and when our fifteen-year-old vacuum cleaner died, he was convinced it was my fault and badgered me to admit that I did something to break them.

—TERRI

Repeatedly putting the partner on the defensive over small things is a way for abusers to fold their power plays into everyday activities.

Another way abusers bolster themselves at their partner's expense is by diminishing their accomplishments:

I had three children under five, including a nursing infant, and decided to wallpaper the kitchen. It took me all day, but I managed to keep the children happy and get the job done. Oh, and I had planned ahead, so dinner was all set to go. I was feeling pretty darn good about myself. When my husband got home, he looked around the kitchen and his only comment was, "You smudged the ceiling. I knew you would."

—TERRI

Being denied well-deserved kudos from a significant other is a demoralizing experience many abused people come to live with.

A partner's confidence and sense of self also get worn down when abusers make a habit of questioning their judgment with offhand comments such as: "Are you wearing that? Do you really think that is appropriate? Is that what you're doing with your hair? Do you really think you should be eating that?" Sierra provides some examples:

He made me feel as though I made bad decisions and I was not smart. If I made a decision about something or bought something for the house, he would find some flaw in it. Then

*he would say, "That's not good. Take it back." Or if I wanted
to do something he didn't want me to do, he would question
my judgment. "Why would you want to do that? That's stupid. Why would you even think about doing that?"*

The abuser's day-to-day negativity creates a toxic environment
that seeps into the partner's consciousness:

*I didn't realize it at the time, but looking back, I heard neg-
ative things so much that I started to believe them. It was
like a hammer and a nail, the more it went in, the more
I believed it, to the point that I thought those things about
myself. It was almost like being brainwashed.*

—CHLOE

When people are exposed to ongoing petty degradations, they
begin to absorb them without realizing it. Eventually their idea of
what is a small offense gets skewed as the abuses gradually increase
in frequency and severity.

IT'S IN WHAT'S NOT DONE

Sometimes abusers show disregard for their partners by what they
don't do, for instance consistently forgetting anniversaries, birthdays, or
other special dates. Not offering common courtesies is another example:

*When we were out in public and saw somebody he knew, he
would start talking to them, but he would never introduce
me. It made me feel like he didn't want people to know me.
Like I wasn't worth knowing, or I shouldn't be in the conversation. It was awkward because people would be looking
at me like, "Who is this girl?" It made me feel like a nobody.*

—CHLOE

Abusers also fail to engage in the simple acts of thoughtfulness that most couples usually do for each other:

> *We both worked from home. At lunch time he would go out and pick up something, but not get anything for me.*
>
> —PAOLA

Or they will decline to show appreciation:

> *I never got compliments. She withheld praise and positive statements. When things went really bad for us, I told her that I had no idea what she actually liked about me.*
>
> —VINCENT

Abusers don't have to openly tell their partners they don't value them to get the message across; they just have to treat them like they don't matter.

IT'S IN THE MANIPULATIONS

Manipulation is subtlety in action. It is an undercover way to get someone to do something they are not inclined to do. For instance, Eaglin wanted more together time with her partner, and he used her request to manipulate her into doing something she found upsetting:

> *I don't like to watch scary movies or shows, but then he would get upset with me. I wanted to go upstairs when he had them on, but he would say things like, "You're so inflexible. You say that you don't feel close to me, but then you don't want to spend time with me. You won't watch what I want to watch." So, we would watch scary, scary shows, and some of them still scare me to this day.*
>
> —EAGLIN

Or abusers may prey on their partner's good nature:

> *She was good at playing the helpless girl to prey on my sensitive nature. She'd say, "Well, I'm just a stay-at-home mom, so I can't do this and I can't do that," which makes it sound like she was making herself vulnerable, but what she was really doing was manipulating me into doing a lot of things she could have and should have done herself. She could turn on whatever she needed to in order to get her way. She was a master manipulator.*
>
> —CQ

One widely used manipulation tactic is the pity party. It happens when an abuser has pushed their partner too far and then realizes they are about to lose control of them:

> *If I had enough and he could sense it, he would start crying, "I don't know what's wrong with me. Something is wrong with me. Maybe I'm depressed or something. I just don't feel adequate." Things like that.*
>
> —Denise

The abuser acts like they are the wounded one in a manipulative ploy to get the person they just harmed to comfort them and make everything okay again.

Denise speaks for many abused partners when she says:

> *I think everything every day was manipulation to make him, one way or another, feel good. Whether we were having a great time together or he was degrading me—whatever made him feel good about himself in the moment. My whole existence with him was a big manipulation story.*

Even though subtle abuses happen repeatedly, they blend in with good times and the simple activities of daily life, so abused partners get lulled into a false sense of safety. Then when their guard is down, there is another blow to their heart, and soul, and psyche. In addition to feeling hurt, diminished, and devalued, they feel deeply discouraged and dismayed that it has happened again.

Although abused partners often feel hurt by the abuser's actions, many of the abusive events are so subtle or seem so small that people question the validity of their own reactions. Not understanding why they feel so resentful, angry, anxious, and/or depressed diminishes their self-confidence and makes it harder for them to tell the difference between emotional abuse and the hard work of relationship.

SUMMARY

- Emotional abuse can be so subtle that abused partners don't realize it is happening.

- It shows up in the abuser's attitude of entitlement and privilege.

- It is expressed through judgmental or rejecting looks.

- Emotional abuse can also take the form of ignoring their partner or their requests.

- It is an accumulation of small slights, put-downs, and other hurtful encounters that get mixed in with daily activities.

ACTIVITY

1. Did you recognize your situation in any of the descriptions of subtle emotional abuse in this chapter? If so, which ones? Have you experienced similar things that are not mentioned here? If so, what are they?

2. Does your partner regularly make decisions that involve both of you without consulting you? Do they consistently minimize or discount your input and go ahead despite your objections?

3. Does your partner have a habit of giving you disapproving, condescending, or rejecting looks? How do you feel about yourself when that happens? How do you feel about your partner when that happens?

4. Are you often frustrated or confused when you try to have conversations with your partner? Do you regularly feel

discouraged by the lack of satisfying communication? After reading this chapter, can you identify what happens that frustrates, confuses, or discourages you?

5. Does your partner repeatedly question your judgment and suggest that you are incompetent or don't know what you are talking about? Do you often feel blamed for small mishaps?

IS IT SUPPOSED TO BE THIS HARD?

No. Strong relationships are marked by an overall attitude of mutual respect, kindness, and consideration. Although people sometimes take each other for granted and forget to give their partners the appreciation they deserve, loving couples show each other they care through small acts of love and thoughtfulness the vast majority of the time.

CHAPTER 6

SUBTLETY PART II

"But Others Have It So Much Worse"

Looking back on the abuse ... although I think that may be
too strong of a word and insulting to people who have suf-
fered traumatic abuse....

—JACOB

I f you are experiencing subtle emotional abuse, you may compare yourself to others who are facing more extreme situations and think that you have no right to complain. Or you may have an idea of what "real" abuse looks like, and what you are experiencing is not that. Please know that just because the abuse is not as bad as you think it could be, doesn't mean it isn't having a detrimental effect on you.

Like breathing the air and drinking the water around a toxic dump, it can do serious damage to your well-being before you know what is happening. In fact, subtle forms of abuse can leave people feeling even more vulnerable and confused than more open forms because there doesn't seem to be any legitimate reason for the profound hurt, unhappiness, and confusion they feel.[14] In addition, when the line between relationship difficulties and abuse is blurred, people often stay much longer, hoping that with a little more effort and understanding, things will get better.

Regardless of its level of subtly, however, all abuse is about having power and control over another person, and by its very nature, a power-over approach to relationship diminishes the other person. In addition, extreme forms of emotional abuse, like raging, controlling the finances, isolating the partner, abandonment or threats of abandonment, and sexual abuse all can be enacted in undercover ways. When these veiled abuses come from a trusted loved one, it adds to the confusion about whether or not they are actually abusive.

EMOTIONALLY ABUSIVE ANGER

Anger shows up in most relationships from time to time, creating tension between couples. It may take several attempts at communicating before the partners find a way to resolve the issue, and the process can be frustrating and distressful. But healthy couples manage to work through the problem and ultimately reach a better understanding of each other, even if they just agree to peacefully coexist on the matter (learning to disagree without being disagreeable). Abused partners usually think they are going through the same kind of process as they struggle to understand the abuser's anger and figure out how to respond.

Emotionally abusive anger is different from the anger expressed in healthy relationships in both its purpose and character. In arguments between healthy couples, anger is usually an expression of frustration at not feeling heard; people are striving for communication and understanding. By contrast, abusive anger is used to silence, punish, and intimidate another person. It is a powerful tool in coercing others into doing what the abuser wants.

Partners frequently use the words "intense" and "terrifying" to describe the abuser's anger. Jackie described how intimidated she felt when faced with her husband's rage, even though he never actually became physically violent:

> *Once in a while I argued with him, but the problem with arguing with him was that it would make him angrier and angrier, and then it would escalate to the point where I felt like he was going to kill me. So self-preservation meant don't argue too much. Throughout the marriage I was careful not to irritate him too much.*

Even when partners don't fear a specific threat, they still feel the intimidation:

*I didn't know what he would do. Not that he would hit
me. He controlled the money. I don't know if he would have
destroyed things. I felt this control. I don't know specifically
what the threat was, but I was terrified. It was something I
couldn't explain. It was the way he looked at me. His intensity.
I had never been yelled at like that before. The way he would
yell at me was like I had murdered somebody, and he was so
mad at me. That was over little things, and it was so intense.*

—SIERRA

Others tell of being backed into a corner, locking themselves in a
room, or finding a way to leave the house so they don't have to face
the full force of the rage coming at them.

Abusive anger is especially effective in intimidating and controlling people who already have a history of abuse, whose self-esteem
and self-concept are fragile, or who have come to believe they deserve
to be treated harshly. Also, there are people who simply don't have
an assertive personality or lack the social-emotional skills to defend
themselves in a conflict with an aggressive person, as Becca explained:

*I wasn't good at the comebacks and the language. I felt over-
whelmed, alone, incapable of defending myself. I was unable
to speak up about how I felt about the situation. It didn't
matter what I said.*

Even for people who come into the relationship feeling strong
and self-confident, dealing with repeated yet unpredictable anger on
a regular basis is exhausting, frustrating, and anxiety producing. It
drains a person's energy and wears away at their self-confidence and
self-esteem, eventually impairing their ability to effectively defend
themselves.

Abusive anger can be so shocking that a person doesn't have to

feel terrorized for it to be intimidating. Even when partners recognize that the level of anger is out of proportion and undeserved,
and they are able to assert themselves, it still takes a toll on their
physical and emotional wellness. Being the target of intense anger,
or even witnessing out-of-control raging, instinctively raises alert
mechanisms in the body. The fight/flight/freeze response kicks in,
causing a racing heart, rising blood pressure, rapid breathing or
holding the breath, and tensing or trembling muscles. As all energy
is focused on the threat, critical thinking is impaired, often leaving the target of the anger unable to think of an effective response.
It can take hours or days for a person to recover from this disrup-
tion to their body and nervous system. Vincent describes the aftereffects of his wife's rages:

> *I will say, when she is escalated, for lack of a better word, it
> is 100% fear, rage, and shouting. Everything is an all-out
> blitzkrieg on everything I am, and withstanding all of that
> is really hard to put into words. It's not like she ever took a
> knife or a hammer, but it is like you are staring in the face of
> something completely alien. The adrenaline surge, the exhaus-
> tion—there were nights when I would just buzz all night
> and the next day. I couldn't sleep and I was just buzzed, like
> a caffeine jittery kind of thing.*

UNDERCOVER ANGER

The high cost of overt, open expressions of anger gives low-level,
undercover anger its power. It is not hard to understand how a person would want to avoid dealing with the shock of abusive anger and
its highly stressful aftereffects. Before long, just the signs that anger is
brewing can be enough for abusers to coerce their partner into doing
what they want them to do, and abused partners gradually begin to

adjust their own behavior in an effort to avoid the physically and emotionally draining experience of abusive anger.

Even if a person is willing and able to stand up to the abuser when they choose to do so, they often will self-censure to avoid a confrontation. Samantha's story shows both the cost of avoiding and the cost of engaging in a confrontation with an emotional abuser:

> *We went to Paris for our honeymoon a year after we were married. He is a very anxious person, and it was anxiety provoking; we don't speak the language. Whenever we walked down the streets of Paris, I wanted to pop in these little stores. He didn't want to pop in anywhere. We had no agenda. We had nothing to do, and he would get irritated. And I said, "I just want to get a couple of postcards...." He was annoyed so I hurried, hurried, hurried—tried to not bother him.*

That "hurried, hurried, hurried—tried not to bother him" reaction becomes a mindset that emotionally abused partners adopt without realizing they are being subtly bullied into complying with the abuser's wishes at the expense of their own. They may believe they are just being considerate or engaging in the give-and-take that is part of any relationship, but when a person regularly constricts their choices, activities, and self-expression because they sense the threat of anger, they are actually being controlled and coerced. Living with the recurrent threat of anger becomes a form of oppression that denies a person the freedom to be who they are.

Emotionally abused partners don't always give into the abuser's implied threat. Many will stick up for themselves when they feel strongly about something. After hurrying to buy postcards so her husband wouldn't get too annoyed, Samantha held her ground about sending them:

Finally, we took the metro to get to the post office because I wanted to send the postcards from Paris. And I said, "Okay, I'm going to hop in here …" and he said, "We don't have time."

"We do have time. I'm just going to go mail these."

"Mail them when we get home."

"We're in Paris. I want to mail them from Paris."

"It's going to cost airmail."

"They're just postcards."

"Why can't you just mail them from home?"

"I want them to see they're from Paris."

We got in a screaming match in Paris outside of this post office. I still went, but when I exerted my power, or said I am doing this, there was such a hefty price to pay. It was so difficult. It shouldn't be this hard to mail a postcard.

When the threat of anger was not enough to coerce her into complying with his wishes, her husband began pressuring her, and when that didn't work, an open and public display of anger followed. An outside observer may judge a person for getting in a big fight over something like a postage stamp, and partners themselves often wonder why they get so upset about such small things. But it wasn't really about the stamps; Samantha was fighting to reclaim a part of herself. Having spent the morning denying herself the spontaneous pleasure of a leisurely stroll through Paris shops because of her husband's irritation, she had reached her limit and didn't want to deny herself any longer. Emotionally abused partners consistently find themselves caught between paying a "hefty price" for asserting themselves or repressing a part of themselves.

UNSEEN EFFECTS OF ABUSIVE ANGER

While abused partners are often judged (by self and others) when they engage in a conflict with the abuser, they also are judged for "doing anything to keep the peace." But those are overly simplistic assessments of the distressing process people go through when dealing with abusive anger. Anticipating, being aware of, choosing how to respond to, and recovering from the abuser's anger all become a nearly constant drain on their emotional, mental, and physical resources. In a matter of seconds, they take several things into consideration as they decide how to respond. Depending on the circumstances, a variety of thoughts may race through their mind:

- Is this worth fighting for? Is this? How about this? How many little things add up to a big thing? Where is the line?

- Do I really want to have this fight in front of the kids, or do I take it again to protect them from another family uproar? What about in front of my family, friends, or in public? Do I stand up for myself when others are there, or give in again to avoid a scene?

- Do I have the energy to engage in a confrontation now? Will I be able to sleep afterward? Focus on my job? Could it become physical? Will it even make a difference? Do I have any chance of being heard? Respected? Solving the problem? What's it going to cost me?

Whether the abuser's anger is open and terrifying or covert and manipulative, it has unseen detrimental effects on the partner.

It Harms the Sense of Self

For instance, when a person chooses to confront the abuser, the resulting conflict is anything but subtle. The subtle part is in how it affects the abused partner's self-image. Phoebe describes how, when she finally found the strength to fight back, it didn't stop the abuse and took a toll on her self-concept.

> *When we would argue, I would know I was right, but his tone and everything would just back me into the corner, and I would kind of start shutting down.*
>
> *I started standing up to him more and more in the relationship, so we got in bigger fights.*
>
> *I cried all the time. I was depressed. I was angry. I was turning into a bitch. We would have arguments in public when we were out on a date with friends. We would be cutting each other down, and I was becoming this awful person.*
>
> *I just got more and more depressed. And it was starting to affect my work.*

When a conflict occurs in public, whether in front of strangers, family, friends, or the children, the abused partner is likely to be seen as "part of the problem." In the struggle to preserve one aspect of herself, Phoebe ended up compromising another. Ultimately, she chose to leave her husband, in part because she didn't like the person she became in her effort to fight for her well-being.

Other people have a very different experience when they try to stand up to the abuser:

> *I tried standing up to him and he yelled louder. It really scared me. I felt like a child. I would shut down, not talk, and would go to my room to cry and sleep.*
>
> —SIERRA

For partners who repeatedly feel overwhelmed by the force of the abuser's anger, self-care in the short term can mean giving in and/or getting away from it until things settle down and seem to get back to normal. On the surface it may look like they've weathered the storm, but their freedom to safely express themselves has been stifled in the process, and a vital part of who they are is lost. Relief at temporarily escaping the abuse masks this loss.

It Diminishes a Sense of Safety

Sometimes, in an attempt to regain a feeling of safety, partners try to minimize the impact of the abuse. Anika shares how she tried to get back to a sense of normalcy after her husband turned discussions into angry tirades:

> *I would try to talk logically with him, "Can we sit down and talk about it?" And of course, he was never in that space, so it always escalated into more fights. There was so much turmoil, and I was just trying to tamp it down, sometimes trying to ignore it. Let's just get through today, go to work and function, take care of the kids. Just try to get through the day and hope it gets better.*

Although the partner has sidestepped the anger, the threat of recurrence lingers. Abused partners eventually find themselves assessing whether any issue they wish to discuss is worth the emotional, mental, and physical cost of another angry onslaught. Consequently, they often let go of things that are important to them, frustrating their efforts at problem solving and infringing on their own enjoyment of life.

When emotionally abused partners can't put an issue off any longer, they will invest a great deal of thought and effort into preventative planning before opening a discussion:

I would let things build and build because every little thing was a huge argument, and it was scary. It was emotional turmoil, and the kids, and everything else. So you tend to let that one go, and let that one go. I would call it the cup filling up. And then finally I'd think, "I can't do this anymore. I can't take this anymore." Then I'd go and talk about it. Literally all day long I would work myself up to say, "I need to talk to you about something," knowing that it was going to be a huge deal. But you don't want to poke the lion, so you wait until, "OK, this can't go on. We've got to have a talk," but it was such a waste of time and energy because it never solved anything anyway.

—Anika

This dread about having the kind of conversations most couples have as a matter of course becomes a significant drain on time and energy that could and should be available for other things. While people in healthy relationships may plan how to present an issue in order to increase the chances of persuading their partner, people in abusive relationships spend time planning on how to bring up an issue without triggering an emotional assault.

It Impedes Self-growth

Because of the unpredictable, unprovoked, and repetitive nature of abusive anger, partners live with a lot of anxiety as they try to anticipate what might come next:

After a while, hours of my time and most of my mental and emotional focus were dedicated to preventively reading her emotional state, with the idea that I could prevent the anger, the rage, the unpredictable moods, and the shouting.

—Vincent

On the surface, partners are protecting themselves, and often their children, from the effects of another display of explosive anger. Underneath that, however, they have been subtly manipulated into protecting the abuser from the need to deal with many of the frustrations, disappointments, and compromises that most adults accept as a fact of life. In effect, the abused person is living in service to the abuser, smoothing their way in hopes of avoiding another distressing episode. In the process, the partner's resources are depleted, depriving them of the energy necessary to appropriately invest in their own self-growth and development.

It Drains Life Energy

In order to preserve some of that energy for other aspects of their lives, abused partners may choose to avoid anything that might spark anger from the abuser:

> *It was so physically and psychologically draining. And I had to function. I had to go to work. I had to do things. And if you already have low self-esteem and low confidence, you are already beating yourself up. So this is just another person adding to that, and you just feel deflated.*
>
> —SIERRA

Abusive anger is intimidating, demeaning, and demoralizing for anyone. It is especially devastating for people who were already struggling with the effects of abuse or other traumas before they got into the abusive partnership. But whether they have a history of trauma or not, the ongoing experience of abusive anger is, itself, traumatizing. Emotionally abused partners often report feeling battered even though they have never been hit.

Frequently they become so worn down and defeated that they

don't have the strength to fight it anymore. Giving in is not so much about keeping the peace as it is about self-preservation:

> *I knew I was going to lose, so it wasn't worth it. If I wanted a peaceful evening, I didn't bring up things. I just went along. I gave up on life. I really did. I would just let him yell; I knew eventually he would stop. I wouldn't bring up any issues. I just didn't have the strength. I was exhausted.*
>
> —SIERRA

In an abusive household, partners are often deprived of a sufficient sense of peace and safety to get the healing rest and renewal that everyone needs to be a healthy, fully functioning individual. The resulting exhaustion not only drains their life energy, but it can also cloud their ability to clearly see what is happening in the relationship.

It Impairs Assessment of the Abuse

In addition to the exhaustion, there are several other factors that can blind someone to the abuse. People undergoing constant stress develop a kind of tunnel vision in which they can only focus on the next step, so abused partners frequently miss the big picture. Since the big picture in emotional abuse often includes times when the abuser is pleasant and loving, the partner is constantly being jerked from one emotional state to another with little or no predictability. Hope and happiness mixed with shock, uncertainty, and despair create a toxic cocktail that throws the abused partner off balance, blurring their thinking.

Many partners start to believe they somehow caused the abuser's anger, or they could stop it if they could just find the right way to handle the situation. They put a lot of effort into trying to figure out what went wrong and how to make it right. In addition, as time goes on, people begin to adapt to their environment, so what is clearly abusive to someone on the outside looking in may seem like "just the way things are" to someone who has been living with it for a while. Jackie's reaction to her friend is a good example:

> *We were visiting my best childhood friend, and she took me aside and said, "Dennis is so mean to you." And I said, "Really? He is?" I had no idea. And I thought, "What is she saying to me? Is he really being mean to me?" I didn't know.*

Another person described telling a friend about an incident that was "*mild—not so bad.*" Her eyes were opened when the friend responded with, "Do you have an exit plan?" At that point she began seeing her relationship in a clearer light. When the abuse is covert and/or the effects are subtle, emotionally abused partners have a hard time believing that they are experiencing abuse.

SUMMARY

- Open expressions of extreme anger can be so shocking and intimidating that after a while abusers only have to look like they are about to get mad in order to get their partners to do what they want.

- Whether the anger is openly aggressive or an undercover threat, it undermines the partner's self-expression, self-esteem, and self-concept.

- Abused partners spend a lot of energy trying to figure out the best ways to respond to or avoid the abuser's anger, and ultimately it takes a serious toll on their emotional, mental, and physical resources, leaving them feeling anxious, exhausted, and disempowered.

ACTIVITY

The following questions will help you identify abusive anger and discern the subtle affects your partner's anger has on you:

1. Do you regularly feel shocked, frightened, or baffled by your partner's anger?

   a. Does it often seem like your partner's anger is an extreme overreaction or is unprovoked?

   b. Do you often have a "walking-on-eggshells" feeling because your partner's moods are unpredictable and volatile?

   c. Have you felt the need to carefully plan and mentally rehearse what you want to say to your partner, hoping to prevent triggering an angry response?

    d. Do you often avoid bringing up issues that are important to you because you don't want to risk facing your partner's anger?

If any of the things on this list above happen regularly, you are experiencing abusive anger.

2. Do you regularly deny yourself small pleasures because of your partner's growing irritation? Do you change your behavior in other ways to avoid a confrontation with your partner? What are they?

3. Do you have a habit of focusing on things you can do to keep your partner from becoming upset? What do you do? How often does that work? What happens when it doesn't?

4. Have you ever stood up to your partner? If so, how often have you:

    a. Resolved issues to your satisfaction?

    b. Given in because your partner became increasingly aggressive or threatening?

    c. Given up because the whole ordeal was just too exhausting, frightening, or frustrating?

If you answered rarely to (a) and often or regularly to (b) and (c), you are experiencing abusive anger.

IS IT SUPPOSED TO BE THIS HARD?

No. In healthy relationships, people can safely have difficult discussions with their partner. Each person still feels safe even when anger comes up. People can express anger without intimidating or silencing their partner, and although it may take some timeouts, working through, or even revisiting the issue several times, eventually each person feels like they've had a fair hearing from the other.

Becca describes how things changed for her after she left a relationship where she was subjected to emotionally abusive anger:

> *With my ex, I was very self-conscious, unhappy, skittish—always looking over my shoulder, wondering if I was doing something to make him mad. I just didn't have that peace that I could relax. I was a much more vulnerable person.*
>
> *Now, I feel whole. I don't have to be skittish. I can be who I am. I have my own opinion about things, and I don't have to mold to what someone else wants me to be. I can just be myself.*

FINANCIAL ABUSE

Financial abuse is about taking control of the money in a way that disempowers and deprives another person. These are all forms of financial abuse:

- Taking money the partner earns

- Refusing access to household funds

- Taking the credit card

- Making the partner ask for money when they need something and deciding whether or not they can have it

- Interfering with the partner's ability to work

- Incurring large debts without the partner knowing or against their will

- Buying or selling stock, real estate, or changing other mutually owned investments without consulting the partner

In addition, many abusers will credibly threaten financial ruin if an abused partner tries to leave the marriage.

Usually, the abuser is the primary wage earner, but not always. Because raging, manipulation, and various forms of retaliation can have a profound effect, there are times when the person making more money is subjected to financial abuse, as Sierra explains:

> I really trusted my ex, or wanted to trust him. So, our money went into one joint account. He paid all the bills. He used to tell me what I could and could not buy. He would monitor my bank accounts and tell me that I spent too much money.
>
> He would make me return things, even if I didn't want to. He would say, "Get up, we're going now!" He wanted to punish

me immediately to say I was wrong, and I shouldn't have done that. Even though he wasn't working, and I was working a couple of jobs. He would go to the store, almost like a parent, "You'd better return this now." And the store employees thought it was weird. They knew something was not right.

He would yell. It was always threats. He never specifically did anything. He might have taken away a credit card. If I tried to refuse, he would make the rest of the evening horrible. He would give me the silent treatment. He would find some way to punish me.

For example, one way he punished her for spending money without his approval was by taking the commuter pass device out of her car. This abuser used anger, intimidation, ordering, public humiliation, and retaliation to enforce his financial abuse.

But it doesn't have to go that far to be abusive. Abusers' attitudes about money can subtly create so much anxiety, confusion, and shame in their partners that they begin to restrict their own expenditures.

In healthy relationships, couples have general agreements about spending and, out of courtesy, discuss unusual expenditures with each other. In an abusive relationship, that courtesy can become an opening for the abuser to assert control. One person describes how her partner used manipulation to shame her about spending money:

It wasn't a problem for me to make routine purchases, and I could draw money from the bank when I needed it, and he could be very generous with things he wanted me to want. But if I wanted something that was important to me but not to him, I would see his shoulders sag and his head drop a little. Or he would do the heavy sigh, furrowed brow, head-in-hands thing, like my wanting to buy something out of the ordinary was an unbearable burden for him. If he finally agreed to what I wanted, he would do it with such a put-upon attitude that it took the edge off my enjoyment. He made such an ordeal out of it that I hated the idea of even bringing up what I wanted to do. I let go of a lot of things I would have done if he didn't make it so unpleasant, which, I guess was exactly the point. There never seemed to be a problem when it was things he wanted, even when they cost a lot more than what I wanted.

—TERRI

Eventually Terri was able to see that her husband's non-verbal behavior was shaming her and deterring her from enjoying the family finances the same way he did. But sometimes people feel the effects of abuse without realizing how it happened:

If I went shopping—like clothes for the kids, or things for the house—I would get so much anxiety about using the charge card, I was shaking by the time I got out of the store. I can't remember why. And he would just go buy something without consulting me. Big things, like the van. We were trying to get out of debt once, and then he came home with a motorcycle.

—ALICE

Making major purchases without consulting the partner is a sign of financial abuse, as are double standards about money matters, breaking agreements about budgets, consistently second-guessing and criticizing the partner's spending, and randomly changing the rules about what are acceptable expenditures. Because money is a major area of disagreement among couples in general, it is easy to mistake subtle financial abuse for the kinds of arguments about spending that occur in many relationships.

SAMANTHA'S STORY

Samantha's experience reveals several forms of subtle financial abuse that easily can be mistaken for the kinds of interactions about money that many couples have:

> *I saw that there was a 50%-off sale at Macy's and thought, "This is great. I need new clothes." I spent $200, which is a lot of money, but I had a whole new wardrobe, which is awesome. He came home, and I said, "You would not believe what I got. I can't wait to show you." I was going to do a whole fashion show.*
>
> *And he said, "Do you need all that?"*
>
> *"Some of the things I really need. I don't need all of them."*
>
> *"Well, what can we take back?"*
>
> *We were making close to $100,000 a year and had no children at that point. He used to call me a spendthrift all the time, and I'm not a big spender. I don't even like shopping. I love a good deal, though. It was very defeating. He would take the wind out of my sails all the time. All the time.*

Remembering that emotional abuse is not about isolated events, but is habitual, the repeated statement, "All the time" is telling. Are there non-abusive relationships where one partner chronically over-spends? Yes. Are they likely to not see it that way and think their partner is being too restrictive? Yes. Is it also likely that spending would be an ongoing point of contention between them? Yes.

This is why looking at the overall pattern is important for discerning whether or not subtle abuse is happening. As Samantha's story continues, a pattern begins to emerge:

> *Another example is complaining about the grocery bill. I was*

clipping coupons, going to three different grocery stores with babies—not an easy task. Going to three grocery stores to save a few dollars when we had plenty of money was ridiculous. And he would say, "Are you crazy? It shouldn't cost this much! Why are you spending so much money?" I'm not really sure why he was doing all that. It wasn't even true. I was trying to be frugal.

Although discussions, even disagreements, about how to reduce the grocery bill happen in many households, there are things Samantha's husband did that were subtly abusive. Her efforts to save money on groceries indicate that the labels of "spendthrift" and "crazy" were name-calling and assigning traits that weren't true. In addition, her husband's questioning of her was not really about getting information and figuring out what to do about the cost of groceries. He was not working with her to solve a money problem; he was badgering and bullying her. Even though Samantha knew her husband was being unfair, his abuse still took a toll on her. She explains:

Financially, I continually got the message that I was a burden.

As abusers' criticisms continue, many partners begin to question themselves, feel shame about their spending, lose confidence in their ability to make good decisions, and constrict their own expenditures. Over time, family finances become a source of ongoing anxiety for them.

In addition, abusers send confusing messages with their double standards. While Samantha's husband was complaining about her spending habits, he was buying concert tickets for himself, and spending money on other things he wanted:

If he went shopping, he would buy whatever he wanted. Not discuss it with me. And then he'd come home, and he would

feel so guilty, I guess, that he would say, "Do you need some-
thing? I spent this much. You can spend that much." And
I was like, "I don't need anything. I don't care what you
spent. Can't we just buy things when we need them? I don't
understand."

This exchange could be mistaken for a discussion about money, and on the surface it may seem like Samantha's husband was trying to be even-handed and considerate, suggesting that she spend something because he spent something. But the key indicator of an abusive attitude here is the idea that he is the one who decides what the criteria is for spending money. Her input, needs, and wants are not part of his equation.

Another aspect of financial abuse is when abusers unilaterally break agreements or change plans without consulting their partner. Ironically, while Samantha was feeling like she was a financial burden to her husband, she also was taking on most of the burden of managing their budget:

I would have all the responsibility and none, or very little,
of the power, and he would have all the power and almost
none of the responsibility. For instance, we would talk about
doing a project on a budget. I did all the research, got every-
thing teed up and ready to go, and then he would say, "You
know what? I'm going to hire someone to do the work." So,
all that groundwork that I laid, all the hours I spent on set-
ting it up was for nothing. That kind of stuff happened a lot
in the marriage, and it was very frustrating.

Home repairs or renovations are notorious for creating conflicts between couples, but Samantha and her husband didn't have a disagreement. He just decided to throw away her plans and hire someone without considering her at all. Not only did he disregard their agreement to work on a budget, but he also dismissed the time and effort she invested in cost-saving measures, devaluing her contribution, and leaving her feeling frustrated, disrespected, disempowered. And, as she pointed out, it happened frequently.

While financial abusers have a habit of being controlling and inconsiderate, they can also be generous when it suits them. In a healthy relationship, gift giving is focused on the loved one. It is a way to say, "I love you. I want to do something nice for you, to make you happy." Ultimately, that was not the message Samantha got from her husband's gift giving:

> *I didn't want any more jewelry. I love jewelry. I love diamonds. I feel special. But the jewelry wasn't about me. I was like a display case for the earrings he bought me. I didn't want it. I felt like he couldn't see me for the jewelry, and I wanted him to see me. It was a very lonely marriage now that I'm thinking about it.*

For abusers, gift giving is usually about their own needs, aimed at boosting their ego, feeling prestigious, putting themselves in a power-over position, or bringing their partner back under their influence. People in Samantha's situation may wonder how it is that they are criticized about spending for clothes and groceries and striving to meet a budget, yet somehow there is enough money for expensive gifts. In addition, it can be very confusing and disorienting when the same person who blocks and frustrates them financially also bestows gifts on them when they choose to.

Another confusing thing about gifts is that people in healthy relationships sometimes bring apology gifts to their loved ones, so it can be hard to tell if an abuser's gift giving is about trying to pull their partner back into the abuse, or if it is an appropriate, caring gesture.

It may take looking at the larger pattern, and/or getting an outside perspective, to determine what is really happening.

A PATTERN OF SUBTLE ABUSE

Although any single incident that Samantha describes might be confused with the typical disagreements about money that many couples have, her husband repeatedly used several abusive behaviors that eventually formed a pattern. He had an attitude of entitlement and superiority that showed up in several ways: the assumption that he was the only one to make decisions about family finances; the idea that he had the right to deny or indulge his partner based on his own whims; the double standard that allowed him to spend as he wished while he expected his wife to defend her expenditures; and his disregard for her opinions and contributions. In addition, when she didn't comply with his ideas of how money should be spent, he resorted to criticism, shaming, name-calling, and badgering.

In short, Samantha's story shows that abusers don't have to do anything as extreme as preventing their partner from working or completely denying them access to family funds to be abusive. They can constrict, undermine, and manipulate their partner using much more subtle methods.

SUMMARY

In addition to the more blatant forms of financial abuse, abusers can use subtle methods that make the abuse hard to discern. Here are some red flags that can help tell the difference:

- One person claims the right to decide how household finances are to be spent.

- There is a double standard that allows one person to spend as they wish while criticizing or shaming the other person's spending.

- One part of the couple has a habit of breaking agreements or changing plans about spending without consulting the other.

- One person regularly makes large purchases without consulting the other.

ACTIVITY

The following questions can help identify subtle financial abuse.

1. Does it seem like your partner has all, or most, of the power to decide how household income will be spent?

2. Do you feel like you regularly need to defend or justify your spending choices while your partner makes purchases as they please?

3. Do you often feel diminished, belittled, or sidelined in family money matters? Does it seem like your opinions and input don't matter very much?

4. Does your partner break agreements or change plans about expenditures without considering your point of view?

5. Does your partner make major purchases without consulting you?

6. Do you regularly feel stress, tension, or fear when you need to talk with your partner about money matters?

7. Do you deny yourself things or activities you would enjoy because you anticipate negative reactions from your partner about the cost, even when it costs the same or less than things they spend money on?

Because the behaviors described above set up an ongoing imbalance of power that puts one person at a disadvantage for the benefit of the other, it is by definition abusive.

IS IT SUPPOSED TO BE THIS HARD?

No. In healthy relationships, couples make agreements about money and how it will be spent. They both have an input, and—for the most part—honor those basic agreements. That doesn't mean there won't occasionally be arguments about finances, but ultimately, they can discuss the issues and come to some kind of accommodation. It may even be that sometimes one person gets their way and another time the other person does, but there is some level of respectful give-and-take between them.

ISOLATION

Isolation is about controlling a person's ability to be in contact with others, especially those who would comprise a support system for them. It can include preventing a person from going to work, school, or other community activities. Sometimes that is achieved by disabling the car or taking the car keys. Another tactic is interfering with communication by taking the partner's phone, computer, or other devices. People may also become isolated because of a move, especially when they move to a place where the abuser has a job and other contacts, but the partner does not.

Abusers can be so intimidating or retaliatory that their partners are afraid to go out against their will, especially when there is no longer a support system to help them. But isolation usually begins subtly and becomes more forceful as time goes on, sneaking up on the partner before they realize what has happened.

IT CAN LOOK LIKE LOVE

For most couples there is a period of time in the beginning of a relationship when they just can't seem to get enough of each other. Early on, they spend every free moment together, and both people may let other activities and connections with friends and family slide for a while.

In healthy relationships, the twosome gradually begins to resume old connections and integrate each other into their broader circle of friends and family. Although they still make their partner a priority and value their time together, they both also enjoy time apart and trust the other person enough to give them space to engage in activities on their own. Abusers motivated by extreme jealousy or possessiveness don't make that transition.

In the beginning, steps toward isolation can even seem like loving actions. For instance, stopping by unexpectedly on occasion can be a sweet romantic gesture. But it can also be a way for abusers to monitor the partner's whereabouts, check who they are with, and monopolize their time:

> *He would come and actually sit in the lobby where I worked waiting for me to get off so we could go home together.*
>
> —SIERRA

This may evolve into stalking behaviors where the abuser is constantly keeping tabs on their partner:

> *He was always tracking everything I was doing, even though I wasn't doing anything wrong. One time I found a cell phone under my car seat that was recording everything I was doing. He would monitor my phone calls and go through my wallet and purse.*
>
> —CQ

Caring couples will ask about each other's day. With abusers, that can gradually turn into expecting the partner to account for their time. Checking in with a partner turns into checking up on them:

> *I would have to give minute-by-minute or hour-by-hour accounting of my days. Repeatedly. So I felt like I couldn't be independent; that I was not trusted, not believed.*
>
> —PAOLA

Partners are often faced with an aggressive third degree, unfounded accusations, and angry reactions when they do even the most mundane things on their own.

Abusers usually begin by coaxing their partners away from their social circle using loving entreaties. Statements like, "I really miss our alone time," or "Let's take time to be just us," are fairly common and appropriate when a couple hasn't had the chance to connect for a while. But when they form a pattern that interferes with friend and family relationships, it could be an early step toward isolation:

> *He didn't want me to do anything without him. If I went to the grocery store, he had to go. If I went to get gas, he had to go. He would always have to be around me.*
>
> —SIERRA

Monopolizing the partner's time to the extent that there is little or none left to spend with others is a subtle way to separate a person from their support system.

When partners assert their natural desire to socialize with others, abusers may become more manipulative and/or aggressive:

> *It was very subtle. He made me feel guilty if I went places without him. If my friends wanted to do an art class or something like that, he would tell me that it cost too much, or the things we were doing were stupid, not good for me somehow. After about a year of being together, he would get angry if I wanted to go do something without him, with any of my friends.*
>
> —SIERRA

Simple outings get turned into power struggles. Sometimes partners feel too intimidated to go out. For those who go anyway, their enjoyment is diminished by the emotional stress of getting around the abuser's objections and the anxiety about what things will be like when they get home.

Sometimes a person becomes isolated after agreeing to move to a different town, state, or country to start a new life with someone they trust as a life partner. That can be an exciting new adventure when the couple works as a team, supporting, and encouraging each other to live this new dream together. With an abuser, the dream can turn into a nightmare. Often the couple moves to where the abuser already has a career and a family/friend network, but they don't integrate their partner into the social group. For example:

> *Once we were married and went overseas, I was stuck. Didn't know anyone, didn't speak the language. It was the days before email, no phone calls, no Face Time. I was totally isolated. He had drinking buddies he would go out with every single night. I'd been home alone all day with the kids, couldn't get out; couldn't go anywhere. So then the fights started, because I started saying, "Well, can't we go out to dinner? Can't we do this, can't we do that?" And then we'd just start fighting, and he would of course blame me, and it would escalate, escalate. Then he would leave, and I would end up being there alone anyway.*
>
> —ANIKA

Whether abusers purposely persuade their partners to move away, or they take advantage of the situation later, the partner is more vulnerable to other abuses once they are isolated.

DRIVING OTHERS AWAY

Another way abusers isolate their partners is by driving a wedge between them and the people in their support system. Sometimes they will denigrate or alienate people in their partner's life, making things so unpleasant for others that they don't want to visit anymore. Or the partner is so embarrassed or anxious about what the abuser might do, they stop arranging social events.

Other times abusers will use manipulation and gaslighting to sow doubts in the partner's mind:

> *He would convince me that my friends didn't like me. He would say, "It seemed like they all went out to dinner the other night. They were talking about that. Were you invited?" And I would say, "You know, I don't think I was." And then he would say, "Oh, well, maybe they're not inviting you," or "Look how they're all talking together at the end of the table. They're not really including you. Do they really want you here?" Those type of things.*
>
> —SIERRA

They will also flip that around and say things to their partner's friends and family to cause a rift between them. Another insidious ploy is to gain the confidence and sympathy of the partner's social circle and create an alliance with them against the partner.

As abused partners gradually lose touch with the people in their lives, abusers typically become more forceful in their efforts to isolate their partners:

> *Over the years, I didn't notice this, but my friends and family became a real problem. There were lots of things wrong with them. She didn't want to see them. They were highly problematic. They were flawed. She didn't want my kids around them. With the result that now as I start thinking about getting support from other people in my life, that number has dwindled down; it is small. There are very few people left. Most have been driven away.*
>
> —VINCENT

Having no support system is a major obstacle people face when they think about leaving abusive relationships.

FOUR LEVELS OF ISOLATION

Being cut off from their support system is only one way emotionally abused people feel secluded, though. They also feel increasingly alone as layers of separation accumulate. There are four levels of isolation emotionally abused partners experience:

1. Separation from others in the community

2. Disengagement from their own interests and activities

3. Disconnection from themselves and their own desires

4. Distance from their significant other

Frequently these levels of isolation overlap and compound each other.

Isolation from Others

Physical separation from others is one of many ways abused partners experience isolation. People can be in regular contact with others and still feel isolated. For instance, when someone can't clearly explain what is happening in the relationship, is too ashamed to share their story, or isn't believed by others in their social circle:

> *It was very gradual. I realized about five years into it that this is not right, and I had to get out somehow. I talked to some friends, but I couldn't articulate it. I couldn't pinpoint it. I wanted to go, but I didn't know why. I couldn't imagine living the rest of my life this way. Then I looked around and nobody agreed with me.*
>
> —Denise

It is devastating and disorienting to people when they feel like something is seriously wrong, but there is no validation of their experiences. They lose confidence in themselves and begin to wonder about their sanity.

Isolation from Activities

Another way partners are isolated is when they are dissuaded or prevented from pursuing activities they enjoy. When persuading isn't enough to keep their partners home, many abusers will resort to ridiculing, guilt tripping, intimidating, or creating some kind of chaos or drama right before it is time for the partner to leave. A person's interests and goals are part of their identity, and when they can't engage in them, their sense of self weakens.

EAGLIN'S STORY

Eaglin had been accepted into two PhD programs when her partner used words of love and concern to convince her to give them up to move away with him:

> *He pursued me really hard in the beginning. He was 31. I was 23. Early on, the way it was packaged—there were subtle pieces. He very gently stroked my face and sweetly said, "I hate that city. Don't you want to be with me?" or "I know how important it is for you to be a mom. How are you going to be a mom if you are in grad school for six years? You want to be a good mom, right?" So, I started feeling confused, because I always knew I wanted to work with kids and be a mom.*

They got married, and she moved to the town where he was already established in his career. There, she got accepted to a third PhD program. Then it was:

> *"Why do you want to get that degree? You don't need that. You don't want to do research ... math is your struggle."*

*And I was like, "I guess not, but I'm …." By that time I was
just really confused because I already was a research assistant,
and I did enjoy it.*

Once Eaglin was separated from her family and the supportive
community at her university, it was easier for her husband to use
their difference in age and life experience to speak as an authority on
her choices. The primary influence in her life, the person she loved,
respected, and trusted, was subtly feeding her undermining messages.
Without counterbalancing input from caring people outside the relationship, she was increasingly susceptible to his manipulations.

Isolation from Self

Eaglin goes on to describe how isolation from others and her goals
led to isolation from her own sense of self:

> *Slowly over time … I didn't see it, but I went from getting
> into an incredible PhD program … then I compromised,
> moved to a state away from my family. Then suddenly I'm
> alone with him in a new city and my world was slowly con-
> trolled. I remember crying, internally crying. So sad, but
> thinking it was the right thing to do to be a good person. I
> didn't look at it as giving up my education goals. I was clear
> that I wouldn't be able to handle it. So he didn't make me.
> I was convinced I couldn't measure up.*

A talented and intelligent person was subtly manipulated into
believing that she didn't have the skills to pursue her dreams. Ultimately, she didn't just lose sight of her goals, she also lost belief in
herself. Abused people can become so beaten down by the abuse they
don't recognize themselves anymore. In addition, the abuse is usually
so undercover that the abused partner can't make sense of their own

reactions. They don't understand why they feel so angry, resentful, anxious, or sad so much of the time. "What is wrong with me?" is a frequent question among emotionally abused people.

Isolation from the Partner

A fourth way people feel isolated is from their significant other when their loved one refuses to make an empathic connection, be supportive, or even communicate.

> *There were times when he was emotionally cold and distant. He would just shut down conversations. He would walk away, or say, "Leave me alone," or lock himself in the office and not come out. He isolated himself. He would ignore me a lot, especially when I had complaints. I just let myself have a more lonely relationship than I wanted. "He just wants alone time. There must be something wrong with me that I don't want to give him alone time."*
>
> —SABRINA

It is no wonder abused partners often say they are lonely, even when they are not physically alone.

Whether abusers use aggressive tactics or more indirect manipulations, the effects of isolation are devastating. Put-downs are more damaging when there are no counterbalancing positive messages. The abuser's denials, blaming, and gaslighting are more convincing when there is no one to provide a reality check. The silent treatment and threats of abandonment are more powerful when the partner believes there is no one else to turn to. With no one to validate their experiences, abused partners feel alone in a disorienting and painful reality.

SUMMARY

- Isolation keeps emotionally abused partners from their support system, making them more vulnerable to other abuses they experience.

- Isolation usually begins subtly and can look like love.

- There are four levels of isolation:

    1. From family, friends, and others in the community

    2. From interests and activities

    3. From self

    4. From the partner

ACTIVITY

1. Did you recognize your situation as you read this section? What parts sounded familiar to you? Did you think of this as abusive before? What do you think now?

2. Does it seem like your partner comes between you and your family, circle of friends, or colleagues? How do they do that?

3. Would you feel emotionally and/or physically safe if you told your partner you wanted to engage in an activity outside the relationship, or spend more time with friends and family? What do you think would happen?

4. Have you stopped doing things that you used to enjoy because your partner dissuaded you or otherwise made it difficult for you to do them? If so, what are those activities and hobbies? How did your partner get in the way of you

doing them? What have you lost by missing out on those things?

5. Do you feel disconnected from others when you can't explain why you are unhappy in your relationship, or they don't seem to understand what you are talking about? What is that like for you?

6. Do you often feel lonely within your relationship? If so, can you discern what leads to that sense of loneliness?

IS IT SUPPOSED TO BE THIS HARD?

No. There is a certain amount of freedom people give up for the benefits of sharing a life with a beloved. For instance, prioritizing a partnership over other relationships is something healthy lovers do, but caring, respectful partners don't expect their loved ones to give up other friendships or family relationships. There is a balance between together time and apart time, and a healthy relationship is enriched by each person's individuality and interests.

ABANDONMENT

Different kinds of abuses build on each other, making them more harmful in combination than they would be alone. For instance, when abusers have effectively used name-calling and put-downs to demean their partners, raging to intimidate them, manipulation and gaslighting to confuse them, financial abuse to limit their options, and isolation to keep them from their support system, then threats of abandonment can be terrifyingly powerful.

Denise, once proud of her independence and professional success, describes her sense of confusion and desperation when her partner intermittently and unexpectedly tormented her with threats of ending their marriage:

> *We'd always grilled out on the weekends. Sit out on our back porch and eat. Things would be great, and then it would be, "You know, I'm just really not happy with you." Out of nowhere something would get triggered, and then the next thing you know I'm across the table crying, because I don't really know what I can do, and thinking, "Oh, my God, not again." So I never knew if he was going to love me that weekend or if I wasn't going to be good enough. I dreaded sitting down with him at dinner. I wondered, "Am I going to feel like I'm about to lose my marriage?" He was constantly dangling that threat in front of me.*

Even years after leaving the abuser, the fear and panic she felt at the time are still palpable. Denise is not alone. Studies show that rejection or abandonment by a significant other elicits pain, fear, and panic in a partner.[15]

People who were neglected, rejected, or deserted by a loved one in the past, particularly in early childhood, are especially susceptible to manipulation by threats of abandonment. Anika describes her internal experience when her partner showed signs of leaving:

> It's like a panic attack. "If you leave, I'm not going to be able to go on." You tie so much into that one person that the thought of them leaving is just devastating. It's like a physical, nauseous, panicked, can't sleep, can't eat thing. It's a very constant heightened fight-or-flight feeling, all this anxiety. "I'll never be loved again. I'll never have another relationship. I'm not OK alone." When I look back, I feel so ashamed.

Her shame was caused by the level of disrespect, disregard, debasement, and physical threats she tolerated to stay in a relationship with someone who was harming her.

EMOTIONAL ABANDONMENT—JAYLA'S STORY

Threats to actually physically leave their partners are only one way abusers use abandonment as a tool of abuse. Emotional abandonment is another way in which they deny their partners a loving connection while still being physically present. Jayla's husband never left or threatened to leave, but he abandoned their marriage by consistently refusing to engage with her. Emotional abandonment was his primary method of abuse:

> When we were dating, we would spend a lot of quality time together. Then after we got married, he just almost refused to spend much time with me. He would never yell at me, or put me down, or get in my face, or threaten me or anything. It was all this very, very covert nastiness.

Although he showed the ability to communicate with people outside the relationship, he steadfastly refused to connect with his life partner. He made a habit of evading conversations when she tried to have discussions. He would walk in a room and act as if she wasn't there, not even looking at her. He regularly failed to be home for the evening meal, and consistently refused to make family or couple time. He even avoided walking beside Jayla when they were out together. And he directly rejected her requests for his company when she asked for it:

> *I remember telling him I like to do out to dinner or go to movies and do social things that weren't outrageous or expensive. There wasn't any reason we couldn't do them. And he'd say, "Well, go do them." And I'd say, "I'd like to do them with you." And he would say, "Well that's your problem."*
>
> *There was never talking, never holding hands. It happened all the time and we would talk about it, so it was not like it was something I was imagining.*
>
> *The loneliness really got to me, that the man I was married to would have nothing to do with me.*

Any one of those rejecting behaviors practiced regularly would be abusive because they deny a person the fundamental human need to connect with their beloved. For Jayla, the ongoing accumulation of emotional abandonments left her feeling not only hurt and angry but utterly bereft. Her profound grief and sorrow at being deprived of any intimacy or connection with her significant other was clear. She ultimately felt so devalued and depressed that she thought of committing suicide.

Realizing that her husband was never going to give her the closeness and companionship she hoped for, Jayla eventually focused her attention on activities with her child, friends, and extended family:

> *It was like I was single, but I was married. I functioned like*

a single woman. I didn't date or anything, but I was always
available if anybody wanted to go to movies or dinner.

While Jayla lived with near total emotional abandonment, it is much more common for abused partners to experience ongoing but intermittent instances of abandonment, mixed in with loving encounters.

Although it helps to have others to turn to, outside relationships don't replace the loss of affection from a beloved[16]. Terri explains:

> *I had friends and confidants I was close to—but it wasn't the*
> *same. Although they were good friends who I could count on,*
> *I wasn't the one special person in anyone's life. The bottom*
> *line was that even though I had people I could talk to, when*
> *I went home to my partner I was still alone.*

Even when a person isn't isolated from their support system, the pain of being repeatedly rejected by a primary loved one is significant.

IT'S NOT ABOUT CONFLICTS

It is important to note that with emotional abuse, the times of abandonment often have nothing to do with a conflict between the partners. Although there are times when walking out or threatening to end the relationship is an angry or manipulative reaction, more subtle forms of emotional abandonment are just a way of life in emotionally abusive partnerships. Marjorie talked about how being abandoned on their honeymoon was only the beginning of how her partner repeatedly left her on her own:

> *On our honeymoon, we stayed with friends of his. We had*
> *eloped so he had done the planning, and he never discussed*

his plans with me. We went to his friend's house for 10 days where he went golfing and left me with a woman I did not know who had a handicapped child. I wish I could say these were isolated events; they were not.

Her new husband was not angry with her. They had not been fighting. He, like many abusers, was just self-absorbed, entitled, and grossly inconsiderate. He went on to abandon his partner in ways that many emotionally abused people will recognize:

- Repeatedly not being there to pick up a partner at the arranged time, or otherwise making them wait for long periods of time

- Planning weekend trips alone without consulting the other person

- Consistently leaving the partner to solve family problems with no support or help

- Refusing to have discussions about the relationship or family issues

- Habitually taking extended time for their own recreational activities while leaving the partner to care for the children with little or no reciprocity

- Not responding when the partner reaches out for companionship or when they are in distress

- Regularly staying out late at night without letting the partner know where they are or when to expect them back

- "Forgetting" to charge or bring their phone with them, or leaving the ringer off, so they cannot respond to calls or texts

- Failing to care for or support a sick partner

- Not recognizing their partner's special days or joining them for their special events

- Having affairs

Sometimes abusers are so self-centered that they just don't consider the other person's needs. They also may be meeting an unconscious need to have distance from their significant other. Or they are purposely trying to manipulate and demean their partner to satisfy their own impulse for power and control in the relationship.

Whatever the motivation, abusers who use these subtle forms of emotional abandonment stay in the relationship but leave their partner over and over again.

SUMMARY

- Threats of abandonment are an abusive tool. They are especially punishing when the partner is already diminished by other forms of abuse and is isolated from their support system, or if they have a history of abandonment.

- Emotional abandonment is a way of leaving the partner while still being physically present. It includes things like not communicating, ignoring, consistently refusing "couple time," being dismissive, taking trips without consulting the partner, staying out late without letting the partner know where they are, or having affairs.

- While outside relationships are helpful, they don't make up for the loss of an intimate connection with a significant other.

ACTIVITY

1. Do you recognize yourself in this section? In what ways?

2. Did you experience abandonment when you were a child? Have you been abandoned at other times in your life? Does your fear of abandonment get triggered in your current relationship? How? After reading this section, do you believe that your partner uses threats of abandonment to manipulate, control, or hurt you?

3. Does your partner threaten separation or divorce in the middle of an argument, or otherwise threaten to leave you in order to get their way, or to keep you unsure of the relationship?

4. Even when your partner is physically there, do you often feel like you are on your own? What are some examples?

5. Does your partner consistently refuse to connect when you reach out to them? What happens when you try to connect?

6. Does it seem like you are mostly responsible for family and household responsibilities that are not part of a mutually agreed-upon division of labor? Do you find yourself needing to make important decisions about the family or household with little or no emotional or other support from your partner? What are some ways in which this has happened?

IS IT SUPPOSED TO BE THIS HARD?

No. In healthy relationships, both people desire the other's company and show it. They each regularly make an effort to spend loving time together. They are emotionally present for each other most of the time.

SEXUAL ABUSE

Sexual abuse, like all abuse, is about power and control. Any non-consensual sex is sexual abuse.

If there are repercussions for saying "No," then saying "Yes" is not consent, it is coercion. All those statements are true even for people in committed relationships.

Sexual appetites between couples don't always match and can change over time; that is not unusual. Even so, loving partners come to some understanding about how to care for each other. Out of love and consideration, one person may engage in sex more often than they really want to, and the other may forgo it more often than they really want to, but love and caring is the primary concern in how they work things out.

Using force or violence is the most easily recognizable form of sexual abuse, but even that can become confusing in the context of an abusive relationship. For instance, when a couple is already involved in a sex act and one partner says it hurts, or they don't like it and want it to stop, but the other continues anyway, it is abusive. Often this happens repeatedly when the abuser begins sex in an agreed-upon manner then switches to something the partner doesn't want. Even within an ongoing partnership, if one person says stop and the other doesn't stop, it is abuse.

SEX, ANGER, AND COERCION

An abuser doesn't have to use physical force to sexually violate their partner. Many partners have sex when they don't want to because they are intimidated by the abuser's anger:

I had sex to make him not be angry.

—Becca

Sometimes the abused person will come to an arrangement with the abuser, so on the surface it seems consensual. But if the person is agreeing to sex to avoid negative repercussions, it is coercion:

> *Sex was in many ways the one time that I felt safe, because I knew that when we were having sex, he was happy. So, I would do anything that he wanted.*
>
> —Eaglin

> *If we did not have sex, he would get very angry. So, I agreed to have sex with him at least twice a week.*
>
> —Leticia

Caring people may sometimes have sex with their significant other when they don't particularly want to because they love them and want to make them happy. That is very different from having sex because of fear or intimidation.

In addition to using anger to intimidate their partners into having sex, many abusers also expect their partners to have sex right after they have been subjected to abusive anger:

> *Then the coercion would come when he was raging. Or after he raged or had been abusive, he would then pretty quickly want to have sex. If I didn't want to he would say things like, "You're withholding affection."*
>
> —Eaglin

Healthy couples often have make-up sex after they have resolved a conflict and restored a sense of mutual affection. Insisting on sex before that reconnection has happened intensifies the abuse.

Abusers also will use shaming, guilt-tripping, ultimatums, or unrelenting pressure to coerce their partners:

He would wake me up and want to have sex, and I very rarely said no, but if I did he would insist on it. "You did this to me, now I'm the one who has to finish it. You just get to roll over and go to sleep soundly, but you get me all aroused, and I then can't sleep all night. You rubbed up against me, and now you just want to sleep. You are so selfish. Don't be surprised if I go fuck other women. That's on you."

Sometimes I did it because I knew he wouldn't let it go until I did, and I needed to get some sleep.

—EAGLIN

People in loving relationships may try to persuade or cajole a reluctant partner to engage in sex, but they don't use put-downs, name-calling, endless pressuring, or threats to get their way.

In the confusion that is typical of emotional abuse, the difference between accommodating a partner and compromising one's own dignity can become blurred:

It is still emotional. It is still raw because I look back and go, "Oh, my God, how did I let myself get that low?" I always felt so dirty and disgusted. I was acting against who I knew I was. One of the psychological side effects of that was I used to shower continuously. I washed my hands and face several times a day at work. I became obsessed with body hygiene, with cleanliness.

—JACOB

Partners often feel shame about the things they let the abuser manipulate, pressure, or coerce them into doing. Shame is not part of healthy sexual relationships.

DENIGRATION AND DISDAIN

Another kind of sexual abuse is showing blatant disregard or disdain for a partner in a sexual context. Sometimes abusers will make it clear that the sex, not the person, is important to them:

> *He tried to position me so he could watch TV and have sex at the same time.*
>
> —Terri

> *We didn't make love very much because it wasn't a very loving relationship. But sometimes we would, and then I would feel really close because of the physical contact. I'd want pillow talk and think maybe now he will pay more attention to me, and immediately he would start ignoring me again. There wasn't any cohesiveness or bonding together over the sex.*
>
> —Jayla

Another abusive tactic is to make denigrating or insulting comments during or after sex:

> *I was really skinny … I carry my weight between my knees and my hips. And every time after we would have sex he would say something like, "You have a good body, and that was good sex, but you have fat thighs." So, he would find a way to strike at me after we had had a very satisfying lovemaking. He did things like that all the time.*
>
> —Phoebe

Terri provides an example of open disdain from her partner:

> *I remember one time in particular. I really didn't want to have sex and he kept at it anyway. I kept telling him I*

didn't want to and cried the whole time. He didn't seem to notice or care. The next morning I told him how hurt and disappointed I was, and he literally sneered at me and said, "You didn't fight hard enough." He was my partner. Why am I supposed to fight my partner? The sneering and the smug, self-satisfied look on his face are seared into my memory. It was like he had some kind of win and was pleased with himself.

Another way abusers denigrate their partners is by grabbing at them in crude and shocking ways:

Early on if I was cooking dinner or unloading the dishwasher, he would come up behind me put his hands down my pants and stick his fingers into my vagina. And I told him, "That is not a turn on for me, dude." Finally, we talked about it in marriage therapy, and the therapist told him to stop doing that. Then he would come home from work and come in to hug me, then squeeze my boobs instead, or grab my butt. Toward the end when he was coming toward me, I would cower and put my hands over my breasts to stop him.

—Leticia

In any other context, those actions would be considered sexual assault, but when it happens in an intimate partnership many people don't recognize it as abuse. Amazing as it may seem, even in the twenty-first century, there are still people who think being in a relationship gives them ownership of their partner's body:

One time he wouldn't leave my breasts alone. I said stop and he said, "They're mine, I'll do what I want with them."

—Leticia

No one is entitled to another person's body, no matter what their relationship is.

IT HAPPENS IN EVERY
GENDER COMBINATION

In addition to women being abused by men, sexual abuse happens in lesbian, gay, and transgender partnerships. It also happens to men in heterosexual relationships.

Vincent described how his wife would change her demands from night to night. She didn't like spontaneity and wanted him to schedule in advance, then she wanted him to be spontaneous, then the room was too hot, too cold, or the lighting was all wrong:

> *Many nights, the weird demands would come so fast and be*
> *so unmanageable that I would get frustrated and just leave.*

Communicating with a partner about sexual preferences is part of a healthy sex life. It is abusive to use a partner's desire to please in order to manipulate them.

While coercing a partner into sex is abusive, so is withholding sex in order to manipulate or punish:

> *We had a massive argument one day. It was atypical in that*
> *I refused to make everything better and take all the blame.*
> *The next morning, she got into bed with me, started kissing*
> *me, had me awake in her hands and ready to have sex, then*
> *she stopped and said, "You need to take back everything you*
> *said yesterday and apologize for making me mad."*

Emotionally abusive women often use shaming and emasculating attacks to abuse their male partners, and men are not immune from body shaming:

Then she'd start telling me that she hates my knees. My knees must never touch her, ever. Then she didn't like my chest, then my shoulders, then something else. Things like that— my body was offensive.

Abusers typically use force, shaming, coercion, and/or pressure to demean their partners. Loving couples typically show respect for their partner's boundaries, preferences, and dignity.

When sexual abuse, abusive anger, financial abuse, isolation, and abandonment are enacted in subtle ways, partners feel the pain and devastation, but they often don't think their experiences rise to the level of abuse. They may see their significant other as a troubled, difficult, and unreasonable person, but they don't see them as an abuser. Consequently, they stay in the relationship, and the abuse continues.

SUMMARY

- Any non-consensual sex is sexual abuse.

- Abused partners tend to confuse coercion with agreement. When a person agrees to sex because of fear or intimidation, they are being coerced. Coerced sex is abusive sex.

- Abusers often use sex to shame, insult, and denigrate their partners.

- Sexual abuse happens between partners in every gender and sexual orientation combination.

ACTIVITY

The following are questions that can help you discern if you are experiencing sexual abuse in your relationship:

1. Has your partner ever used physical force during sex that was not part of a consensual scenario?

2. Has your partner ever continued a sexual act after you said you wanted them to stop?

3. Have you ever had sex with your partner to avoid their anger or other forms of retaliation?

4. Has your partner ever used shaming, guilt-tripping, or ultimatums to get you to engage in sex when you didn't want to?

5. Have you ever given in to sex because your partner wouldn't leave you alone until you did?

6. Has your partner ever used sex to show disregard or disdain

for you? Have they said insulting or hurtful things to you in a sexual context or just after being intimate?

7. Has your partner ever withheld sex to manipulate or denigrate you?

Any one of these behaviors is sexually abusive.

IS IT SUPPOSED TO BE THIS HARD?

No. People in healthy relationships hear and honor their partner's "No" even when they want to have sex. And though they might be disappointed, they are not vindictive. Mutual care and consideration guide sexual interactions between loving couples.

CHAPTER 7

DENIAL

"Am I Going Crazy?"

I went into therapy and the first thing I said to my thera-
pist was, "I think I'm crazy. I must be going out of my mind
because here's how I feel and here's what I'm told is going on,
and these two just don't reconcile. I must be nuts."

—Vincent

D o you sometimes find it hard to make sense out of what is happening in your relationship? Do you frequently feel thrown off
balance? If your partner makes a habit of openly denying that hurtful thing that just happened, you may often feel shocked and confused on top of the hurt.

Or maybe your partner uses denial in a more undercover way. How
would you know? One sign is that you have started to feel less and less
sure of yourself since you have been in the relationship. You're not as
confident as you used to be. You've started to question yourself more.
Like Vincent, you may even be questioning your sanity. Emotional
abuse tactics are often disorienting on their own. When denial of
the abuse is added to the mix, it can create a crazy-making situation.

Denial is not just an abusive tactic; it is an integral part of the
abuse process.[17] Abusers not only deny their own abusive actions,

but they also add to their partner's pain by denying their experience of the abuse as well. In addition, denial is built into certain abusive practices such as blaming, gaslighting, and passive-aggression.

Gaslighting happens when the abuser denies the partner's experience of reality; it is an attempt to undermine a person's confidence in their perceptions, judgments, sense of self, and even their sanity. Passive-aggression is an undercover way for someone to harm another person while denying what they are doing. Let's look at all of these in greater detail.

GASLIGHTING

Denial of Feelings

Probably the most common use of gaslighting is when an abuser tells their partner that their feelings about a hurtful event are not legitimate. The abused person's objection to being treated badly is cast as a character flaw with statements like, "You're too sensitive." That simple statement (and its more aggressive variants such as "You're too uptight, too paranoid, too high drama, too high maintenance, or just plain crazy") packs an abusive punch that hits home on several levels. Because of that denial, the abused partner will likely feel any or all of the following things:

- Frustrated because the abuser refuses to take their complaint seriously
- Diminished by the denial of their feelings
- At fault for complaining
- Ashamed about being too sensitive
- Confused and self-doubting (Am I overreacting? Am I wrong to feel this way? Is it okay to be treated this way? Is something wrong with me?)

Since the phrase, "You're too sensitive" seems benign on the surface, many abused people can't make sense out of where that cluster of negative feelings is coming from. In that fog of uncertainty, the abuser's statement gains credibility, and partners wonder if they really are overreacting or expecting too much. Consequently, they are increasingly at risk of accepting more abusive treatment.

Another abusive aspect of the "You're too sensitive" denial is that the phrase contains a conversation-stopping message: "My behavior is not the problem, your feelings about it are, but you are wrong to feel that way, so there is nothing to talk about, and I refuse to discuss it." In addition to everything else, the abuser's denial disempowers the partner by unilaterally shutting down communication.

Denial of Perceptions

Abusers also use gaslighting when they habitually deny their actions by saying things such as, "You misunderstood; that is not what I meant, not what I said, not what I did, not what happened. You're crazy, you're making things up, you're imagining things. I wasn't sarcastic, I wasn't angry, I wasn't condescending. You are way too sensitive and imagining things."

Or they may act oblivious and look at their partner with disbelief saying, "I have no idea what you are talking about." Sometimes abusers will openly deny doing what they are very clearly doing:

> *He would look over other women when we were out together,*
> *even turning around to watch them walk away. When I con-*
> *fronted him about it, he said I was imagining things because*
> *I was insecure and I just needed to get over it.*
>
> —MARJORIE

Even if the abused partner is not convinced or confused by the abuser's denials, they are shocked and baffled about how to respond to someone who refuses to acknowledge an obvious reality.

In another confusing tactic, abusers deny the abuse by simply ignoring that it has occurred. In a particularly head-spinning maneuver, abusers will strike an emotional blow, and then go back to a pleasant, loving attitude with no explanation or acknowledgment of what just happened. For instance, moments after a tirade they will suggest going out, or they'll bring their partner a cup of coffee as if nothing had happened. The switch from abusive to loving leaves the partner feeling unsure how to respond:

> *My husband would come to me for a hug after he had just treated me badly. I think it was his way of apologizing. He had just yelled at me or done something mean and instead of saying sorry, he wanted a hug. I had no idea how to respond to that. It felt so strange. It didn't seem right to push someone away who wanted affection, but I hated it when he did that. It felt like a violation, but I couldn't name it at the time.*
>
> —TERRI

Confronting an abuser who is actively denying the abuse usually results in more denial and an escalation of abusive anger:

> *He just got done screaming at me and breaking dishes, and telling me I'm a piece of shit, and things like that, and then an hour later everything would be fine. And he would want me to think it was fine. The best thing I could do was to make it feel fine if I wanted it to stop.*
>
> —BECCA

The threat of renewed abuse subtly coerces the abused partner to join in the denial of what just happened to them, which constitutes yet another level of abuse.

Blaming

Abusers often deny responsibility for the abuse by blaming the other person for causing it. If their partner would only comply with the abuser's wishes, then there would be no need for anger, threats, or other kinds of retaliation:

> *It was always my fault. I was the one who was doing wrong. The only reason problems existed was because I did this, or that, or whatever.*
>
> —Denise

Another way abusers use blaming is by denying that they are the abusive one and claiming their partner is the real abuser:

> *He was yelling so loudly his face was red and the veins in his neck were bulging. I locked myself in the bathroom. He started pounding on the door and saying that I was abusing him because I was withdrawing and not communicating with him.*
>
> —Anika

And when abused partners directly confront their abusers, they often get this kind of response:

> *You're the one who is abusing me because you're making me feel so badly. How do you think it feels for me to look in the mirror and have to remind myself that I am not a monster? You say you're being abused, but you're taking that away from people who really are in danger. You've never been in danger.*
>
> —Eaglin

Abusers also will project blame onto their partner by accusing them of doing what the abuser is actually doing. For example, a person who is having affairs will accuse their partner of being unfaithful, or someone who regularly has fits of rage will say their partner has an anger problem.

In addition to blaming the partner for the abuse, abusers will also blame their partner for other kinds of issues:

> *She lost her job, and somehow it was my fault, even though I didn't drive her to work or get her the job. I didn't have anything to do with the job. She would do anything not to have to look at herself. I was the closest person to her, so anything she didn't want to take responsibility for automatically fell on me.*
>
> —ELLEN

If there is a kernel of truth in the abuser's accusations, or if they are persuasive enough, the partner may begin to wonder if they deserve the blame that is being foisted on them:

> *He got a traffic ticket for speeding and blamed me for it because he said I was distracting him. He was so adamant that it was my fault that I was convinced he believed it, so I questioned myself. Was I at fault? Did I distract him? Maybe we could take the blame together for it? But that was out of the question, too. It was fully my fault.*
>
> —WARREN

Abusers can become so forceful in their denials and false accusations that the real issue becomes lost in a highly charged uproar that blocks rational communication and leaves the partner in an emotionally battered and disoriented state.

PASSIVE-AGGRESSION

Passive-aggressive behavior allows abusers to strike a blow at their partners while plausibly denying what they did:

> *For the first several years of our marriage, we only had one car, and my husband did not like sharing it. If I had to use it for some reason, usually a doctor appointment, I always—and I mean always—had to wait for a long time when I went to pick him up. This is a man who was into routine. Unless there was a traffic problem, he got home within a ten-minute window, but when I was waiting for him in a downtown parking garage—summer heat or winter cold—it was at least a forty-five-minute wait. That was true from my first pregnancy until after the third child was born. In the end, I was waiting forty-five minutes or more with a nursing infant, a toddler, and a preschooler in the car. When I brought it up in couple's therapy, both my husband and the therapist acted like I was nutty to think he was doing it on purpose.*
>
> —TERRI

When partners call abusers on their passive-aggressive behavior, the abuser typically not only denies it, but often acts wounded that the partner would accuse them of doing such a thing. So the abused partner is doubly harmed: not only receiving an invisible hit that is then denied, but they are also framed as the offending person.

Abusive Joking

Another passive-aggressive tactic is passing mean comments off as a joke. The abuser denies the comments were intended to be hurtful and blames the partner for not being able to take a joke. Abusive joking is hurtful whether it happens in private or in public, but in public it takes on added dimensions. A good sense of humor is a widely appreciated attribute, and not having one is considered a social deficit. So the abusing partner gets to look like the fun one, while the abused partner is caught between accepting the humiliation or looking like a stick in the mud who just can't take a joke. But laughing with someone is quite different from laughing at them:

> *I was lactose intolerant, and he would make fun of me in front of other people for my GI stuff. I felt so ashamed. Then he would say, "Give me a break. You're being so dramatic."*
>
> —EAGLIN

Here's another example:

> *"I was just teasing you. You get so weird about these things. I probably shouldn't joke with you because you take things so seriously." Then he would laugh.*
>
> —WARREN

Abused partners may question their own reactions and wonder if there is something wrong with them for not finding the joke funny. In addition to the shame of being the butt of demeaning comments, they may also feel shame about not having a good sense of humor.

In healthy relationships, both people enjoy the joke. Caring partners avoid topics the other person is self-conscious about. If a partner does overstep a boundary, they sincerely apologize and steer clear of that kind of joking in the future. There is no hard and fast rule about jokes; what is funny to one person may well be hurtful to another. The person who is the object of the joke gets to decide, and a respectful, loving partner will honor a request to refrain from hurtful humor.

The Stealth Attack

The stealth attack is a passive-aggressive ploy where the abuser strikes at a raw nerve in the partner by saying something hurtful in public that is only understood by the two partners:

> *My mom cooks very well, but her rice is not that good. That is the only thing she doesn't cook very well. So one comment I will never forget is … a friend of his was visiting, and I made soup with rice. The friend was complimenting my soup, saying, "This is a great soup. Oh, my gosh, this is so delicious." And my ex said, "Yeah, the only thing you cook like your mom is the rice." I was getting a compliment and he turned it into an insult about my cooking."*
>
> —PAIGE

For the abused partner to object or react to one of these covert blows in front of company would be socially unacceptable. The abuser gets to either land an invisible punch with impunity, even appearing good natured while doing so, or succeeds in provoking the abused partner to a seemingly irrational response.

THE PARTNER'S DENIAL

Some abused people accept mistreatment because they were raised in abusive homes and don't know there are healthier ways of being in relationship. That is not denial. Denial is when someone sees the red flags and, for whatever reason, chooses to ignore them and continue with the relationship:

> *He was very controlling even at beginning of the relationship. I wanted to break up with him after a month because I thought it was odd that he lost his job, his car, and was almost evicted from his apartment. He had several of his friends convince me that he was a good stable person. I wanted to believe them, so I stayed.*
>
> —SIERRA

People mention a variety of reasons for overlooking the red flags. They may think they won't have another opportunity to have a life partner; they may think they have to settle because they don't believe that they can do better or deserve better; they may hope that with time they can love their partner better or otherwise change the things they don't like about them; or they may think the good outweighs the bad, among other possibilities.

Once in the relationship, abused partners often echo the abuser in rationalizing the abuse:

> *I would feel hurt a lot, but I didn't necessarily see it as abuse. I always found a reason for it. He treats me that way because of what I did, or because of what he is dealing with, or he can't help it because he had a tough life. He doesn't know how to love. It is not his fault.*
>
> —BECCA

Partners who make excuses for the abuser's behavior, often in the name of being understanding and compassionate, don't realize that they are inadvertently enabling them to continue the abuse.

Often partners get so caught up in the routine of daily life that tolerating the abuse seems like a reasonable trade-off:

> *I worked and brought in more money, but he was doing a lot of work at home, and I couldn't have had the job I did if I didn't have that support at home. So, there was a lot of, "Just get through the day. I'll think about that tomorrow."*
>
> —ANIKA

In the business of getting from one day to the next, the reality of the abuse can get pushed to the side of consciousness.

Another reason people deny what is happening is because they love their partner. They want to see the best in them and hold onto what is good in the relationship:

> *I think I was trying to justify him subconsciously because I didn't want to lose him, and I didn't want him to be that person. So, I was thinking maybe it's something I'm doing. Maybe I could do something different. Maybe he'll change. Maybe all that will go away. But it never did.*
>
> —WARREN

Sometimes the denial is motivated by shame and intimidation:

> *She hid it, and I helped her by not telling anyone, by lying in the rare instances when someone did notice; I felt compelled to keep the peace, prevent more rage. I suffered the most for these choices and for the silence that I enabled.*
>
> —VINCENT

It is helpful for abused partners to become aware of how they have used denial in the relationship so they can make more conscious choices going forward:

> *I had to look at myself and what my part in it was—the acceptance of someone treating me in a way that I didn't agree with is not the way to go.*
>
> —BELINDA

People who left their emotionally abusive relationships share some insights:

> *Denying to yourself that it is actually abuse and trying to justify it is not a good thing. Always giving the abuser a way*

out—we need to stop that. We get red flags. Quit denying that those signs are accurate and real.

—ANIKA

Pay attention to the signs. Don't sweep things under the rug. If something makes you uncomfortable, or makes you feel less-than, there is validity there. Don't keep brushing it off because it is not going to change. Not without real help. We can't change people. Don't take things so lightly.

—BECCA

While abusers use denial to minimize their own responsibility and harm their partners, the partner's denial usually leads them to harm themselves in order to minimize the abuser's responsibility. Either way, the partner pays a heavy price for the denial in an abusive relationship.

Denial can make it hard to tell the difference between emotional abuse and the hard work of relationship in at least two ways. First, the abuser's denial undermines the partner's confidence in their own perceptions, so they become increasingly unsure of themselves and their ability to accurately assess their situation. Consequently, they become more susceptible to the abuser's manipulations. Secondly, the partner's denial not only minimizes the reality of the abuser's harmful behaviors, but it also minimizes the reality of the harm it is causing themselves.

SUMMARY

- Denial is an integral part of the abuse process.

- Abusers habitually deny responsibility for their actions and put the blame on their partners.

- Abusers use gaslighting and passive-aggressive behaviors to confuse, hurt, and undermine their partners while denying they are doing so.

- Abused partners often deny or minimize what is happening in the relationship and make excuses for the abuser.

ACTIVITY

Make a list of the ways in which you feel confused and frustrated in your relationship. Look back to see if the source of that confusion and frustration is related to the tactics described in this chapter. The following questions may help you discern if denial is occurring in your relationship:

1. Do you regularly hear: "You're too sensitive," or "You're overreacting," or similar statements when you bring a complaint to your partner?

2. Does your partner often claim that what you are complaining about never happened? Or do they frequently say you just misunderstood when their intention was quite clear?

3. Does your partner repeatedly ignore that they have done something hurtful to you and act as if everything is fine?

4. Does your partner have a habit of blaming you for their

hurtful actions, saying if only you hadn't done such and such, they wouldn't have treated you badly? Do they blame you for other things that are clearly their responsibility?

5. Does your partner regularly do undercover things that are hurtful to you, but are easily denied?

6. Do they say hurtful things, and then claim they were joking?

7. Do they make stabbing comments in front of others that only you get?

8. Looking back, do you think you have ignored red flags in your relationship? Can you identify reasons why you ignored them? What did you gain from the denial? What did you lose?

9. On a scale of 1-10, where is your level of self-confidence compared to where it was before this relationship?

IS IT SUPPOSED TO BE THIS HARD?

No. Jackie shares an important perspective from her therapist:

I was starting to feel nuts, and I thought, "Oh, I'm crazy. I'm just crazy." And I was told, "No, you're really not crazy. You're living in a situation that's making you feel crazy. So you have situational depression and anxiety." And I began to realize I wasn't mentally ill. I was just in a really bad situation that was making me feel mentally ill.

In contrast, Paige describes how things are different in her new relationship with an emotionally healthy partner:

My current partner is very rational. He tells me, "This is what is going on. This is what you are saying to me. This is how I feel." So I can see and clearly understand, "Yeah, that makes sense." And I don't think it is my fault, and he doesn't throw it back on me.

CHAPTER 8

TELLING THE DIFFERENCE

"Could This Be Emotional Abuse?"

I thought we just had some quirks that needed to be worked out.

—Anika

I was telling my therapist and my close friends what was going on, so I started to get the message that stuff was happening, but I wasn't really aware of it. I had no idea that it was emotional abuse. I thought it was normal.

—Jackie

Have you, like Anika and Jackie, spent a lot of time believing that your relationship is pretty much like most relationships, but there are just some issues—bumps or quirks—you need to work out? Are you beginning to wonder if that is true? Can you tell the difference between "all relationships have their problems" and a problem relationship?

It is true that you can't expect people to be perfect, but how do you tell the difference between accepting someone's faults and accepting abuse? How much hurting is too much?

How do you tell the difference between emotional abuse and the hard work of relationship?

Several elements make it hard to discern between the difficulties most couples face from time to time and the ongoing hurt and confusion that comprise emotional abuse.

To review:

- First there is the partner's mistaken assumption that both people are participating in the same loving relationship contract based on mutual care and support, without realizing that abusers have a compelling need for power over their intimate partners.

- Next, much of the abuse is masked behind a veil of subtlety, and the more open abuses are explained away through various kinds of manipulation and denial.

- Finally, adding to the confusion is the fact that couples in most relationships sometimes do things that hurt their partners, and many abusive relationships also have some positive aspects. It can be very difficult for a person living in the middle of it to know which is which.

HURTFUL EVENTS HAPPEN REGULARLY

While it is helpful to know that hurtful events happen regularly in abusive relationships and only occasionally in healthy ones, it can still be difficult for abused partners to figure out where the line is. How often is "regularly?" Several times a day? Once a day? A few times a week? What about a few times a month?

John Gottman (2018), a marriage therapist who has observed communications between thousands of couples over the course of decades, offers some guidance. He reports that, "Couples whose love lasts have a ratio of 5 to 1 positive to negative interactions during a fight or conflict. When they are just hanging out, they have a ratio of 20 to 1 positive to negative interactions" (p. 217). Whether your relationship reaches those thresholds or not, it is safe to say that *loving couples share an overwhelming majority of positive exchanges over negative ones.* People in strong relationships regularly express appreciation, affection, and affirmation toward each other. Abusers may do some of those things some of the time, but the positive times are randomly mixed with recurring disregard, disrespect, and disdain.

MARKERS FOR EMOTIONAL ABUSE

Some signs of emotional abuse are easier to identify than others. For instance, name-calling and put-downs; constant criticism and negative comments; unfounded jealousy and stalking behaviors; threats and menacing actions; and anger that seems unprovoked, disproportionate, or unexpected are some of the more obvious markers. However, some abuses are harder to identify because they are very subtle and/or they blend in with everyday interactions.

Abuse can be discerned in the abuser's self-serving and controlling behaviors, their ongoing disregard for their partner, their manipulations, and their refusal to communicate.

MARKER 1: THE PARTNER'S REACTIONS

Let's look first at how the abused partner's internal reactions can indicate emotional abuse.

The Partner's Gut Reactions to Abuse

One marker of emotional abuse is the internal reactions partners feel on a regular basis, reactions that are not typical of people in healthy relationships. When people describe their experiences with an abuser, they often use words like shocked, stunned, disoriented, baffled, devastated, and heartbroken. Emotionally abused people will recognize themselves in many of the following comments:

> *When it started, I was just shocked. And I would cry. I remember a lot of crying. I think I used up all my tears in those years.*
>
> —ANIKA

> *I felt emotionally put through the ringer.*
>
> —ABIGAIL

> *I felt loneliness, fear, depression, anxiety, doubt, low self-esteem, embarrassment, shame, judged, little, unintelligent, like a child being scolded by a parent.*
>
> —BECCA

> *I felt constricted, boxed in.*
>
> —CHLOE

> *I felt trapped and controlled, like I was in prison.*
>
> —JAYLA

> *It was like walking on eggshells. Not tripping him off was my North Star.*
>
> —EAGLIN

> *I never felt like I could let my guard down with her.*
>
> —PETE

> *I never knew what to expect. He was predictably unpredictable.*
>
> —ALICE

There was always a feeling of trepidation when we needed to have a discussion.

—Vincent

I felt overwhelmed, incapable of defending myself. I felt alone. There was a heavy sadness, a lost feeling.

—Ellen

I remember thinking I was lonelier when I was married than I was before I was married.

—Marjorie

Not feeling valued. I didn't feel like I mattered. I was such a disappointment.

—Paola

I felt inferior, stupid, lazy, fat, and insignificant. He sucked the energy out of me. It was exhausting.

—Sierra

A gradual saddening for myself, and losing myself and who I was, and losing joy, spontaneity, and overall comfort, and being able to relax without being on edge.

—Leticia

It was like being shell-shocked. I felt zoned out, in a trance.

— Terri

I felt like I was dying a little bit more every day. And I knew I just couldn't survive. I would not choose to survive. And I also

*had this feeling that if I stayed very long, I would end up being
so completely compromised that I wouldn't be able to leave.*

—PHOEBE

Although most people occasionally feel hurt, frustrated, and angry
with their partners, they rarely, if ever, have the kinds of deeply traumatized feelings described above.

The Partner's Reactions In a Healthy Relationship

By contrast, the following comments are from people who left
an abusive relationship and found a very different experience with
a loving partner:

*I feel loved. I feel like I belong. I feel spiritually connected. I
feel whole. I feel good about having a whole life and being able
to express myself without fear of abandonment and rejection.*

—ALICE

*I can be who I am. I have my own opinion about things, and
I don't have to mold to what someone else wants me to be. I
can just be myself. I don't have to check in everywhere I go. I
actually want to call him and let him know what I am doing.*

—BECCA

*I can speak to people and look towards someone and not be
accused of being interested in them.*

—WARREN

*I don't get yelled at for making decisions. It's a mutually
respectful relationship.*

—SIERRA

I can be vulnerable with him. I can express all of my emo-
tions with him. He is my rock.

—CHLOE

After my husband left, I was depressed. I had no idea what
was going to happen, and I would cry out of nowhere. This
new guy I was seeing, he would just hug me for half an hour.
He would say, "It's ok. You are going to be fine." It was exactly
the opposite of someone ignoring me and playing a video game.

—PAIGE

He sees me. He's there for me. I can count on him. We're not
at odds all the time. He respects me. He's considerate.

—SAMANTHA

It was all so hard back then. I was always trying to fix what-
ever it was I thought was making him angry. And it's funny;
with my husband now, it is so easy.

—ANIKA

Abused people may have some of the above experiences some of the time, but if they happen, they are regularly mixed with subtle and not-so-subtle abuses that repeatedly take the partner back to hurt, confusion, and/or anxiety.

MARKER 2: A HABIT OF IGNORING

Yet another marker for emotional abuse is ignoring. Abusers ignore promises and agreements; ignore boundaries; ignore it when they have hurt their partner; ignore meeting times—leaving their partner waiting for long periods of time; ignore requests for help, cooperation, or compromise; and ignore their partner when they reach out to connect.

Many emotional abusers habitually ignore their partner's attempts to communicate. They will avoid eye contact, act preoccupied, or otherwise show disinterest in what the other person has to say. In caring relationships, both people participate in the communication process:

> *The biggest difference is that we actually communicate. It's a two-sided conversation. That's the key to our relationship. We talk about everything. I think that's the foundation of why it works.*
>
> —JACOB

Loving couples show their interest by making eye contact, and engaging responses like nodding and making empathic facial expressions. They give feedback like, "Mm-hmm," or "I get that." When appropriate, they ask questions to get a better understanding of what their partner is saying, or just to show they care:

> *Now that I'm with my new partner, I see how normal people do it. If I start to feel uncomfortable about anything, I can talk to him. We sit down and talk and he says, "Are you okay now? Are we good? Are you feeling better? Is there anything else we need to talk about?"*
>
> —ANIKA

People in strong relationships may not always agree or understand each other, but they feel heard and respected most of the time. Repeatedly being ignored when trying to reach out and connect is a sign of being emotionally abused.

MARKER 3: ONE-SIDEDNESS

Another marker for emotional abuse is the different ways in which abusers and caring partners approach everyday aspects of their relationships. Mutuality and reciprocity mark healthy partnerships, while one-sidedness is a sign of an abusive one. For example, in abusive relationships, one partner tends to think of the other's needs and wants while the other is self-focused:

> *You try to see it from their point of view—they've had a bad day, their job is tough, they need some down time. But in all of these, I'm not part of the equation. My stuff gets put last. And if you're with someone who is self-centered and thinking only of themselves, you'll always be last. It should never be one-sided like that.*
>
> —SAMANTHA

By contrast, in mutually respectful relationships both people are actively engaged in making the relationship work:

> *Now I can build a healthy idea of what love is and what it looks like to have both people making an effort. It's mutual, both people doing things, being honest, not hiding things, not having ulterior motives.*
>
> —CHLOE

Loving couples make a habit of showing care and concern for each other. Abusers made a habit of focusing on their own wants and needs, often at their partner's expense.

Unilateral Decision Making

Decision making is another way to distinguish between mutually supportive and abusive relationships. Considerate partners usually consult with each other about decisions that affect them both. Abusers regularly make unilateral decisions without regard for the impact on their partner:

> *My ex would make decisions all the time, make plans all the time, never consulting me, so it wasn't a reciprocal reliance there. Now, my partner and I make very few decisions without consulting each other. We get feedback from each other. Working together as a team is just a natural part of our relationship.*
>
> —Jacob

That sense of teamwork is a sign of respectful relationships. Abused people often feel disregarded and dismissed by their partners.

MARKER 4: MANIPULATION

Manipulation and gaslighting are part of emotional abuse, but they can be difficult to spot for the person who is being subjected to them. One telltale sign is the effect it has on a person:

> *Pay attention to your confusion. It is your greatest indicator. In my healthy relationships, everything is so different. Sometimes I needed to figure things out, or it was hard to open up about my feelings, but it wasn't confusing. I knew where they stood. The confusion wasn't there.*
>
> —Eaglin

> *It is a whole different world to be with someone who actually cares about you and genuinely loves you and isn't trying to manipulate or control you.*
>
> —Chloe

Because of the confusion, abused partners often lose self-confidence as the relationship continues.

Dr. Jekyll/Mr. Hyde Behaviors

The Dr. Jekyll/Mr. Hyde pattern of behavior is another confusing aspect of abuse, but it is a little easier to identify than other kinds of manipulation. Being kind in public but unkind in private is one sign. Another is unpredictable behavior: abusers can quickly go from pleasant to mean in ways that baffle and stun their partners. Anxiety and confusion about what is going on between the couple is not a regular part of healthy partnerships, but it is a marker for emotional abuse.

Sabotaging Problem Solving

Abusers are especially averse to communicating when their partner brings a complaint or attempts to solve problems in the relationship. They avoid talking about issues by deflecting, blaming, gaslighting, walking away, or simply refusing to acknowledge what the other person has to say. Mutually supportive couples have discussions that move toward understanding and problem solving:

> *In my marriage, the arguments went to, "Why are you bringing this up now?" He would put up a wall and accuse me rather than ever addressing the issue. So we would have arguments that were never resolved.*
>
> *But now, with my fiancée, we have very productive arguments. In fact, we always try to work toward resolution and try to make it so that we don't have to argue about this again. We are really, really trying to understand what it was that caused the problem so that we don't do it again.*
>
> —JAYLA

Far from reaching an understanding, abused partners often come away from conversations feeling more hurt, frustrated, and alone then when they started. A recurring sense of rejection and frustration when trying to solve problems with a partner is another sign of emotional abuse.

Sabotaging Therapy

Many abusers refuse to go to couples therapy, and those that do often use manipulation to sabotage the process. For instance, just as they use the Dr. Jekyll/Mr. Hyde approach among family and friends, they also use it in therapy:

> *I watched this guy whose was a raging tyrant at home turn into the Pillsbury Doughboy in the therapy office. He acted utterly clueless and baffled by my complaints. He said he'd never heard them before, even though for years I had tried every way I could think of to get him to understand. Once, he framed my complaint about some controlling behavior as me being a feminist who objected to traditional male courtesies. When we left, I asked him if that was really the way he saw it, and he said, "No."*
>
> —TERRI

Or they will be agreeable in the office then ignore or sabotage the therapist's suggestions:

> *We went to three different therapists, spent a lot of money on therapy. And we would walk out of the therapist's office, and nothing would change. One time the issue of affirmations came up, and the therapist gave a homework assignment, "Before you come back next week give her three affirmations." And as we were walking out to the car, he gave me three superficial affirmations. It enraged me that he didn't seem to want to try.*
>
> —JAYLA

While most emotional abusers will subtly minimize, deny, evade, and misrepresent the relationship problems in order to avoid dealing with them in therapy, others will blatantly lie:

> *We went to couples counseling after a huge argument. When we got there, my wife gave this sweeping catalogue of every single thing I had ever done wrong. Some of it was a real reach and that lasted for about an hour. It was so bizarre and so far outside of anything I've ever experienced. When I brought it up later she said, "You're so stupid. I made all that up. I did it on purpose." Then, with a straight face, she denied she ever said that.*
>
> —Vincent

Therapy is hard work, and resistance is sometimes part of the process, but people who value their partner and the relationship will make an honest effort to do the work.

Denial

Another form of manipulation, and an additional source of frustration for abused partners, is the abuser's denial. When someone consistently shuts down communication about a problem by claiming that what happened didn't really happen, or that the partner's perceptions and feelings about what happened are wrong or invalid, it is a sign of emotional abuse:

> *When I went to him about things that bothered me, he told me it was all in my head. I was not believed. I was not heard. I did not have a voice for years.*
>
> —Marjorie

Considerate partners are willing to hear their partner's complaints and take them seriously:

In my current relationship, I could be really angry with my partner and come tell him that I was really angry with him, and he'd just listen. He would want to know more. He wanted to know why. He cares about my feelings.

—Sabrina

When someone consistently denies responsibility for their harmful actions, it is a sign of abuse.

HEALTHY RELATIONSHIPS ARE NOT PERFECT RELATIONSHIPS

Expressing Anger

There are times when people in otherwise happy relationships have disagreements that aren't easily resolved. They get angry and sometimes they yell. The difference in yelling between caring partners and the yelling that is part of abusive anger is that most people yell out of frustration when they feel like they are not being heard. Although it is not the best method of communication, the goal is still to communicate. Even during a conflict there is a two-way exchange. In healthy relationships, people eventually back up, calm down, and try again when the air has cleared a bit.

In contrast, abusers use anger and yelling to silence and intimidate their partners. Abused people often feel overpowered, afraid to express themselves, or so frustrated by the futility of trying to be heard that they give up. Most significantly, the conversation doesn't continue after things calm down because the abuser's ultimate goal is to stop the communication:

Now that I'm in a healthy relationship, I've learned a lot. I used to withhold a lot of my feelings and anger. I kept it all in for years. Now I'm able to express it. There is a safety

component with my present husband. I feel like I can be
myself, and I can take my space if I need it.

—ALICE

"There is a safety component" is a revealing comment. *People in healthy relationships feel emotionally safe with their partners, even when they are in a conflict.* Abused people often find that confronting their partner intensifies the aggressive reactions, and communication deteriorates even further.

Some Examples of the True Hard Work of Relationship

Ideally when people have an argument, they focus on the facts of the problem and avoid name-calling. But sometimes people don't handle conflicts as well as they would like:

Yeah, sometimes we'll say things like, "You're an asshole, I'm not doing this right now," or whatever, and walk away. But we always come back and talk about it when we're calmer. Always. We don't just come back and say, "I'm sorry. I'm sorry too." We also actually talk about what happened, and what brought that on…. Feelings: why did that hurt so much?

—PAOLA

Part of the true hard work of relationship is resisting the very human tendency to become defensive when someone brings a complaint. Warren provides an example:

I can go to him about anything. If I tell him about something he did that hurt my feelings, he might become defensive. With him, when he is doing that, it is because he is feeling really bad about it, so he's trying to justify to himself why he might have done it. But we can have a conversation about it, and it will all come out.

When he brings a complaint to me, "You are doing this," I want to say, "Well, you do it, too." I want to say that. But I've learned not to, because that's not opening up dialogue. That's just throwing mud over the fence at each other. So, it is very hard. We can talk about me doing that, then after the conversation has gone on for a while, I can say, "And you know, there are times that you do that as well." I can bring it in, but way down the conversation instead of just throwing it right back at him.

Warren is describing a process of hearing his partner out before responding with his own reactions. Putting the brakes on the impulse to deny or lash out is an example of the true hard work of relationship, and in respectful partnerships, *both* people strive to do that.

Sometimes the hard work of relationship requires a partner to admit when they have done something hurtful:

Sometimes we do place blame on each other, but we don't carry on with it. Either she will apologize, or I will apologize, whoever really is at fault. So, sitting down and having a tough discussion—communication can be very hard and uncomfortable sometimes, but we have learned that it is necessary.

—ELLEN

Emotionally mature adults can muster enough humility and honesty to acknowledge that they have done something hurtful, offer a heartfelt apology, and make amends as appropriate.

Another example of the true hard work of relationship is navigating a way through conflicting needs:

*We have opposite attachment needs. I get my needs met phys-
ically; she gets her needs met emotionally, so there is a lot of
compromise and doing work that is below the surface, which
really shows how committed we are to growing and being successful in the relationship. I tell you, the last thing I want to
do is be emotionally vulnerable, because I just have such a
strong resistance to it, but I'm learning to make myself vulnerable again, and she is not using it as a weapon.*

—ELLEN

Taking the risk to trust again when a previous partnership has
been hurtful can also be part of the hard work of relationship. Loving couples respond compassionately to each other's vulnerabilities.
What they don't do is expect their partner to accept mistreatment
because of their own painful past. *Healthy relationships are emotional
as well as physical safe havens for both partners.*

What all these examples have in common is the willingness of
both people to have respectful and empathic conversations, even
when it is difficult:

*Everybody's got problems. You work on them together. You
have to be honest about what those things are, and sometimes that's hard. It took a lot of awkward, honest conversations to get to this point. Communication is the biggest thing
that resonates with me.*

—CHLOE

In strong relationships, couples make two-way communication a
priority. Emotional abusers are masters at not communicating. They
habitually shut down conversations and avoid solving problems with
their partners.

SUMMARY

While it is often difficult for people in emotionally abusive partnerships to recognize what is happening, there are some markers that
can help them tell the difference between a healthy and an abusive
relationship. Caring relationships can be identified by the following
characteristics:

- Reciprocity instead of one-sidedness

- Mutual consideration and teamwork instead of unilateral
  decision making

- Open, honest encounters instead of manipulation and
  gaslighting

- Behavior that makes sense to the partner instead of hurtful Dr. Jekyll/Mr. Hyde-style switches

- Attentive, caring engagement instead of ignoring

- Taking responsibility instead of denial and blaming

- Joint efforts to resolve issues instead of sabotaging problem solving

- Striving to keep lines of communication open instead of
  shutting down conversations

ACTIVITY

The following questions will help you tell the difference between
emotional abuse and the hard work of relationship:

1. Look at the examples of gut reactions emotionally abused

people experience on page 200-202. How many of them apply to you? Do you experience those things regularly?

2. Does your partner habitually treat you with disregard, disrespect, and/or disdain? What are some examples? What effect does that have on your self-image and self-esteem?

3. Does your partner often ignore you? Do they consistently ignore promises and agreements they have made with you?

4. Is your partner's approach to the relationship marked by mutual care and consideration, or do they have a habit of looking out for their own interests at your expense?

5. Do you often feel confused and unsure about what is happening in the relationship? Is it hard to get straight answers from your partner when you ask them about their confusing behaviors or statements?

6. Does it seem like your partner sabotages your efforts to improve the relationship by derailing attempts at problem solving, by gaslighting, or by unilaterally ending conversations?

7. Do you have a recurring sense of rejection and frustration when trying to solve problems with your partner?

IS IT SUPPOSED TO BE THIS HARD?

No. Three people who left abusive partners and then got into healthy relationships give their perspective on this important question:

I don't think you are supposed to work so hard at a relationship. It does require some work, obviously; you've got two people with different lives that are intertwining, and there is going to be some work there, but it's not supposed to be difficult. It's not supposed to be a daily struggle. It's not supposed to be living in fear of, "If I say something, are they going to explode on me?"

—WARREN

Good relationships are easy, like the relationship you have with your best friend. They can really be that easy. If you and your significant other understand each other and have basic communication skills, the relationship doesn't have to be hard. Your partner should not be the source of conflict in your life. Your partner should be the person who helps you deal with conflict coming in from the outside world.

—SABRINA

You'll know it is healthy when it empowers you instead of diminishing you.

—JACOB

CHAPTER 9

NORMALIZING

"How Could I Have Let That Happen?"

I can't believe I was such an idiot. It took me a long time to forgive myself for allowing that to happen.

—Paige

A friend I'd known for years told me about a couple of people she knew who had similar things happen to them. One of them is quite famous as a healer. She said, "It can happen to anyone. It is not just you."

—Porchia

I wish I forgave myself earlier and learned to love myself earlier, because that would have helped. Working on my self-worth was vital.

—Alice

Do you know that people typically judge themselves harshly when they realize they've been in an abusive relationship, just as Paige did? And like Porchia, their shame is reduced when they learn that they are not alone, that even prominent, successful people can be abused? Does Alice's discovery that self-forgiveness is a vital part of healing from abuse surprise you?

Judith Herman (1992), a widely renowned expert in the field of trauma, explains the importance of addressing shame and judgments in the process of recovering from abuse: "A frank exploration of the traumatized person's weaknesses and mistakes can be undertaken only in an environment that protects against shaming and harsh judgment. Otherwise, it becomes simply another exercise in blaming the victim" (199).

Negative judgments diminish self-worth, and low self-worth interferes with the healing process. When abused partners begin therapy, get into a support group, or otherwise communicate with people who understand emotional abuse, they find that they are not alone. They discover that there are many similarities in the circumstances that make people vulnerable to abuse, in their reactions to the abuse, and in the ways they come to terms with the abuse after they realize it has happened. With increased understanding, abused partners judge themselves less and respect themselves more, clearing the way for them to develop the confidence and strength they need to begin the healing process.

UNDERSTANDING JUDGMENT IN ABUSE

Judgments are pervasive in abuse. Abused partners are judged by the abuser, by people outside the relationship, and by themselves. Often, the most severe self-judgment comes when they realize they have been in an abusive partnership. Vincent's reaction is typical:

> *Once I realized what was going on through therapy, I thought, "I must be the dumbest man ever. I must be the stupidest idiot in the world to go along with this for so long. I wasted so many years of my life."*

For some people, the realization is more gradual, and the judgment is marked by the confusion that so often accompanies emotional abuse. For instance, it is not unusual to hear, "I can't believe I was so stupid," within a few sentences of, "Maybe I'm making a mountain out of a molehill."

In addition, people sometimes swing between judging themselves for staying and then judging themselves for wanting to leave:

> *There was judgment about wanting to leave. Why is it I want*
> *to abandon somebody? Why do I want to quit my partner?*
>
> —ABIGAIL

Many abused partners also feel, or expect to feel, judged by people outside the relationship, so there is a sense of shame about letting others know what is happening:

> *I didn't see it for what it was, and then when I did, I thought,*
> *"Who do I tell? They are going to say, 'Why did you stay? If*
> *you see it now, why didn't you see it then?'"*
>
> —DENISE

That fear is not entirely unfounded. The subtlety and duplicity that confuses abused partners can also deceive others. And the unfortunate truth is that abused people are often judged no matter what they do. They are judged for trying too hard, for not trying hard enough, for not seeing it sooner, for complaining about what they do see, for accepting the abuse, for confronting the abuser, for staying, for leaving, for forgiving, or for not forgiving:

> *The same people who defended my partner and judged me*
> *for complaining about my relationship were also the ones*

who judged me the most for staying once they got what was
really going on.

—TERRI

Even though it can feel scary to reach out, the healing effects of support from understanding others make it worth the risk. Most abused people who get into therapy have found that it is a life-changing experience. For people who can't find help in their immediate community, the National Domestic Violence Hotline (see page 297) is a good place to find non-judgmental support. And, yes, emotional abuse is a type of domestic violence.

UNDERSTANDING THE POWER OF VALIDATION

Although abused people often reach out to others to talk about their pain and confusion, they rarely recognize that their relationship is abusive. It is usually a friend, family member, coworker, or therapist who first gives a name to what the partner is experiencing:

My friend said, "How much longer are you going to take this
abuse?" And that comment was the beginning of me escaping
because it had been labeled. Labeled for what it was.

—JACOB

Sometimes a person is not ready to hear that information:

I did not tell anyone what he did as I was a very private
person. I realized he was controlling, and I did not want to
admit that I was being controlled. I was afraid to be judged
or shamed. I was afraid to leave, so I did not want anyone
to convince me to leave as that frightened me.

—SIERRA

If a person is still in denial, they may become offended at the suggestion of abuse and defend the abuser. That, too, is part of the process for many people. But if they are ready, having someone identify the abuse can be either a shocking eye-opener or a welcome confirmation of their sense that something is wrong:

> *Some friends pulled me aside and said, "Can't you see what he is doing to you? You need to get out of this relationship." And they told me what they saw. Then I was able to see it clearly, "Wow, I really am being abused. It's not just me." I was never sure my perception was real.*
>
> —PAOLA

Recognizing the abuse is the beginning of change for many abused people:

> *That was my turning point because people understood. People believed. Suddenly, I wasn't alone in this. For me that validation was sort of a release. I was ready to let go at that point because I realized that this is really happening, and people know it now.*
>
> —WARREN

The best antidote for judgment is the validation, support, and encouragement that comes from connecting with empathic others. If an emotionally abused person does not have this level of support in their own circle of family and friends, or even if they do, they may find therapy or counseling, whether individual or group, extremely empowering and healing.

UNDERSTANDING THE
FAMILY OF ORIGIN AND ABUSE

Many abused people feel a drop in self-judgment when they realize how their family of origin experiences left them vulnerable to
abuse in their adult relationships. Because little children depend on
their caretakers to get their basic needs met, they learn to adapt their
thinking and behavior to accommodate abusive family members.
Often their safety depends on appeasing the abuser and responding
with passive, if anxious, compliance. In order to make sense of their
lives, they become accustomed to rationalizing the abuser's behavior.
Frequently, their rationalization is that they are bad and deserve to
be mistreated. In addition, children tend to believe that what happens in their household is the way things are supposed to be, so they
come to accept abuse as a fact of life:

> *That's what kept me from identifying it as abuse, because it
> was so nitpicky and small in my mind. Now looking back on
> it, there was some pretty big stuff I allowed. It started with
> my upbringing. It was just the undertone of my entire life,
> so I didn't realize how big these things were because they'd
> always been there. You get used to it.*
>
> —Jacob

Another way children get primed for abuse in adult partnerships
is when they are required to take on responsibilities that are not
appropriate for a child. Young people in that situation learn that
they are expected to focus on the needs of others at the expense of
their own:

> *I realize now that I was always trying to protect my mother.
> I was always trying to make her happy. Then my mom was
> always hiding in her bedroom, and I was with my brothers.*

It's only because I've gotten help that I can look back on it now
and see how that contributed a lot to me taking the abuse.

—DENISE

Giving of the self is a religious and social value that gets skewed in the context of emotional abuse where people get the message that they do not have the right to take care of their own wants and needs. Abandonment also predisposes children to accept abuse:

I think having my dad leave so early made me very clingy
and needy, that whole abandonment thing. Clinging onto
any relationship. Not believing that I was good enough to
be on my own or good enough to have someone treat me well.

—ANIKA

People who fear abandonment are especially susceptible to manipulation and coercion by an abuser who will threaten to leave if their partner doesn't comply with their demands. In addition, a strong sense of dependence and fear of being alone makes it harder for the abused person to end the relationship.

Because of their early training, people from abusive families usually miss the signs of abuse that others can see because they have been conditioned to overlook or accept them:

I grew up in a very dysfunctional family. I thought the sit-
uation I had in my relationship was better than that, so of
course I could live with it.

—BELINDA

Even when families aren't abusive, people rarely escape childhood without some kind of wounding that shapes their future behavior:

I came from a cohesive family. But my mother was extremely dominant, and the coping strategy I developed was, "It doesn't matter what you think because it is going to be overridden anyway." So I learned to be very passive and accommodating. I emerged from my childhood without a very good self-concept and not knowing how to take care of myself. I just always assumed it was my fault. Because of how I had to deal with my mother, I never could really advocate for myself.

—JAYLA

And it is not only relationships with parents that influence a person's behavior in future partnerships. Highly aggressive or bullying siblings can also have an impact:

My brother was a relentless bully. My mother treated it as typical sibling rivalry, but he was older, smarter, and stronger than me. I could never win, and he only got meaner when I tried, so I learned to make myself small, be invisible, and stay out of his way. When my husband started to bully me, I didn't believe I could stand up for myself. I'd never been successful at it. I didn't think I knew how.

—TERRI

Sometimes it is the overall family dynamic that influences a child's self-image:

I grew up in such a large family that I would get lost. I was not used to having a voice. My voice didn't matter.

—MARJORIE

I had very poor self-esteem. I was in need of attention and approval. I tolerated a lot of things that are intolerable because I wanted to be accepted. I wanted to belong.

—ALICE

Understanding how their childhood prepared them to accept abuse helps people develop more self-compassion. "When survivors recognize the origins of their psychological difficulties in an abusive childhood environment, they no longer need to attribute them to an inherent defect in the self" (Herman, 127).

Another benefit of understanding how early childhood experiences influence adult relationships is that instead of falling into old patterns, people can begin to make more conscious choices about how to interact, not only with a partner, but in relationships of all kinds.

UNDERSTANDING MYTHS ABOUT ABUSE

There are a lot of misconceptions about what causes abuse. Abusers, abused partners, and often society at large believe that abused people do something to make the abuse happen. It is important for partners to know that whatever faults and weaknesses they may bring to the relationship, they do not deserve to be mistreated. The abuser alone is responsible for their harmful behaviors.

Vulnerabilities and Faults Don't Cause Abuse

Many abused partners believe that their vulnerabilities cause the abuse. They don't. They make people more susceptible to abuse, but they don't cause it. Loving couples try to create a supportive, encouraging environment that brings out each other's strengths. Abusers will exploit their partner's weaknesses for their own benefit. Chloe explains how her partner used her anxieties to isolate her and take control of her life.

CHLOE'S STORY

Chloe came from an unstable family where there was domestic violence and substance use. She, understandably, entered her relationship with anxiety issues. Despite her difficult home life, she was popular at school and felt good about herself among her peers. Then she met Richard, who gradually started isolating her from her friends:

> *I didn't realize it in the beginning. We were teenagers, so I didn't realize he was jealous and controlling. He wanted to go through my phone, didn't want me to talk to people, didn't want me to go out anywhere. At the time, I mistook jealousy for someone caring about me.*

Chloe's adolescent naivete and trust made it possible for her boyfriend to manipulate her, but it didn't cause the manipulation. Given her home life, control felt like caring to her.

Chloe and Richard married. Once she was isolated from her family and friends, her husband further magnified her anxieties and isolated her. For instance, when they went out, he wouldn't introduce her to his friends or do anything to include her in their activities, all of which increased her anxiety in public. Then he used gaslighting to convince her that she was too anxious to go on outings:

> *I wanted to go to a festival that was coming up. I had an extreme phobia of bees. I tolerate them now. He would say, "Oh, that's probably not a good idea. We'll be outside and we'll probably see a bee. Remember that time you saw a bee, and you started crying? You embarrassed yourself in front of all those people." Then I felt shame and didn't want to go. He would act like he was being helpful or nurturing, but he was really using it against me to get out of taking me somewhere or doing something for me.*

As the isolation and undermining continued, Chloe's anxiety grew, and she became more dependent on her husband. He would exaggerate her fears as an excuse to leave her home alone while he regularly went out and enjoyed time with his friends, often staying out until the early morning hours, causing her to feel afraid and worried:

> *The situations turned into "You owe me" scenarios. "Remember what happened last time? Remember about your anxiety? So just think about the things you might run into. I know you get freaked out around people. I think you owe me. I deserve to go by myself." Then I would stay at home. He would be gone for hours and hours and not answer my texts. Sometimes he wouldn't come back until three in the morning. By that time my anxiety was so bad—you know, you imagine the worst. So, he might come back at three in the morning, and I was so panicked by that time. I'm crying. I'm worried. And he comes in and says, "Don't worry, I'm fine." And then he'd give me a hug, and I was so starved for affection and attention I thought that was a good thing. "Oh my God, he hugged me. This is great."*

With her husband's emotionally abusive treatment, Chloe's anxieties eventually developed into traumatic bonding and agoraphobia:

> *The way that he treated me led to me essentially becoming agoraphobic. I absolutely would not leave the house. I did not believe the world was for me, and I was too afraid to go out.*
>
> *I got jobs when he kicked me out, or when I moved away. But any time I would have an amount of success, he would come back and then I would lose it and have to start all over again. I was never able to work when we lived together.*

Chloe had some anxiety before she started her relationship with Richard, but she was still able to enjoy a social life at school. And when they were separated, she was able to overcome her fears enough to get a job and make some friends. Chloe's upbringing and anxieties didn't cause her husband to abuse her, but it did make her vulnerable to someone who wanted to have control over her life.

Chloe eventually got outside support and gained enough strength to permanently leave Richard. She later met a partner who values and cares for her. Thankfully, she discovered another way to be in an intimate relationship:

> *Everybody's got baggage, everybody's got problems, and you work on it together. I've definitely learned a lot about how a relationship is supposed to work. Now I never feel hidden. I don't feel like I'm supposed to be ashamed of myself. I feel like I'm important. He wants me around. It is such a huge difference. That feels so great. It has been so beneficial for me to look at what love is and is not.*

Mental Health Issues and Addictions Do Not Cause Abuse

It can be difficult to live with someone who is dealing with mental health issues such as phobias, depression, or obsessive-compulsive tendencies, among others, but abuse is never a justifiable response. Loving partners will balance their own self-care with care for their partner and do their best to create a safe and encouraging environment. And when old wounds are not constantly being reopened by current abuses, people are better able to progress in their healing process. While people with mental health issues are responsible for getting the help they need to increase their wellness, they are not responsible for the actions of an abusive partner.

Addiction is another issue that creates problems in relationships.

But just as an abuser's addiction does not justify abuse, neither does an addicted partner deserve to be abused. A healthy partner will set boundaries that an addicted person won't like. But they won't use threats regarding the addiction to coerce a partner into doing things that are harmful or that keep them in an abusive situation:

> *Our relationship was very much correlated with substance use. We were using a lot of different substances, then we graduated to heroin, and at that point she just had a lot of stuff that she held over my head. So, if I would want to leave, or try to leave, she would threaten me with telling my family, the authorities, anything she could think of. It was scary. So, that was a big factor in my staying.*
>
> —ELLEN

Sometimes recovery from addiction and recovery from the abuse happen in tandem:

> *And I just hit a breaking point where I said, "I will take whatever repercussion it takes to get away from this." It had gotten that miserable. I felt more empowered when I got to rehab. I was getting my life together and making the changes I needed to make. When I went to get help—I think that is when it really hit me, when the reality of the abuse set in.*
>
> —BECCA

Addictions and mental health issues complicate relationships. When healthy partners don't know how to cope with those difficulties, they turn to professionals for help. They may even choose to end the relationship, but they do not use their partner's weaknesses to further harm them.

Disagreements and Differences Do Not Cause Abuse

Abused people are inclined to believe they deserved the abuse because they did something that irritated their partner:

> *If I didn't say that, he wouldn't have reacted. If I didn't act like that, then he wouldn't have reacted. If I would only be more fun, things would be better.*
>
> —ANIKA

It is not that abused people never do anything that is legitimately annoying to their partner; of course they do. That is the nature of being human. But even if a person is completely at fault for a particular incident, abuse is never an acceptable response:

> *I have a counselor today who lets me know that no matter how difficult or demanding I may be, I do not deserve to be treated that way. Like dealing with relentless sarcasm and name-calling when I bring up things he doesn't want to talk about.*
>
> —SABRINA

Disagreements and conflicts happen in relationships. It doesn't mean that a partner is "asking for it" or that they deserve ill treatment:

> *I have learned that it is OK for me to make mistakes, but it is not okay for me to let someone take advantage of me or be ugly or cruel to me.*
>
> —BECCA

There are ways to air complaints and set boundaries without resorting to abusive tactics. Mutually respectful partners engage in a constructive give and take to address their problems. Irritations and conflicts are part of most relationships; abuse is not.

UNDERSTANDING HOW ABUSE CREATES VULNERABILITIES

In addition to the vulnerabilities people bring into the relationship, the abuse itself creates vulnerabilities in the abused partner. Emotional abuse has a significant negative effect on a person's mental and physical health.[18] It lowers self-worth; increases self-doubt; affects a person's ability to concentrate, make decisions, and problem solve; and leads to high levels of anxiety, depression, suicidality, and Post Traumatic Stress Disorder.[19] Some emotional abuse survivors have described the effects the abuse had on them:

I can think of two times when I actually had a plan for suicide. I couldn't do it because of my children. I needed to stay for them even though I really didn't want to be here anymore.

—TERRI

I have struggled with depression off and on. Throughout my entire marriage I was on medication. Now I am on the lowest dose of my antidepressant. I have definitely gotten my life back since leaving. I am so happy right now, it is amazing.

—LETICIA

I internalized all that anger, and it came out in panic attacks and phobias. I had what someone might call an emotional breakdown, and had a hard time functioning, so I started therapy.

—JACKIE

I started being obsessive-compulsive. I was cleaning all the time. I couldn't control much, but I could control the little things around me.

—PAOLA

I had PTSD (Post Traumatic Stress Disorder), mood swings and crying spells. I questioned my own decisions.

—ABIGAIL

The symptoms started slowly for me. Then they were progressing and becoming more severe. I sat down at my computer to do my job and started crying and couldn't stop. Memory loss and forgetfulness got really bad. My anxiety was so bad I was having irrational thoughts. I remember feeling so timid and so vulnerable at points that I was almost out of body. I remember driving to a function and feeling vertigo.

—HALLIE

In addition, the high levels of stress and sense of disempowerment that accompany abuse often lead people to adopt coping methods that cause them even more harm:

I numbed my feelings through the use of drugs.

—BECCA

I used eating to numb myself. I became a workaholic. I cried a lot in private.

—SIERRA

I cut myself.

—PAOLA

I picked up alcohol to go to sleep and not think about it

because I couldn't shut my head off. Then I realized that I
was just making things worse.

—DENISE

The mental distress and detrimental coping methods create another
layer of shame in the abused partner.

People who are clear that they did not cause the abuse still
feel diminished and disempowered by the emotional assaults they
experience:

> *I knew I didn't deserve it. And I knew it was totally out of*
> *proportion. I knew it was his baggage, not mine. But I was*
> *overwhelmed. I was tearful. Why was he doing this? Why was*
> *this happening? Even though in my mind I knew it wasn't*
> *about me, I still internalized it because it was so painful. I*
> *felt inadequate, and weak, and vulnerable, and depressed,*
> *and irritable. I could cry at the drop of a hat.*

—PHOEBE

Even when a person enters the relationship feeling strong and
confident, they can still develop mental and physical health vulnerabilities due to the abuse.

In addition to the mental health ramifications, abuse can also lead to
stress-related physical ailments such as chronic pain, lowered immune
function, elevated blood pressure, heart disease, inflammation, obesity,[20]
headaches, ulcers, spastic colon, and gastro-intestinal problems:[21]

> *My hair started to fall out. I was having trouble sleeping. I*
> *got these rashes on my face. Hot and cold flashes. I noticed*
> *an increased heart rate. Digestive issues—I was either having*
> *diarrhea or I was constipated all the time; there was never*
> *a regular cycle for me. I lost weight.*

—HALLIE

Abusers often express disdain for the very problems triggered by the abuse, and will use those vulnerabilities to further exploit, undermine, and demean their partners.

UNDERSTANDING THE
STAY-OR-GO STRUGGLE

Judgment also arises around the abused person's struggle with the decision of whether to go or stay. It can be helpful for partners to know that because of the fundamental human need to bond with a significant other, the reluctance to end an intimate relationship is nearly universal.[22] This is often true even for people experiencing abuse: "The fact that people resist breaking off an attachment that causes pain attests to how deeply rooted and powerful the need to belong is" (Baumeister, 503). Belinda describes the process she went through in deciding to end her relationship and the anguish she felt after leaving:

> This was the progression for me. My first inclination was, "I can deal with this. I married him. I can live with this." Then it got to the point where I said, "I don't have to live with this." Then it was, "I won't live with this." Then I left. Then I believed I ruined my life—that's how I felt at the time. And I tried to move on, but he was still the person I cared about, so I wasn't moving on. I wasn't growing. So, my lack of accepting the inevitable—that it wouldn't work—prolonged my agony.

Leaving an abusive relationship is often fraught with confusion and ambivalence:

> The last three or four months, we didn't have much of a relationship because I was trying to avoid him. It was weird. I didn't want to leave him, but I didn't want to be around him. I arranged my schedule to avoid being at home when

he was there. That was my way of leaving him without actu-
ally taking that step.

—WARREN

For some people, the shock of recognizing the abuse is enough for them to start proceedings to leave. For many others it is a more gradual process. They see the need to end the relationship before they have the wherewithal to take the necessary steps:

I think I've already said twice, "That's when I knew I had to get divorced." That doesn't mean I took action. Deciding to get divorced was different from finding my strength.

—SAMANTHA

Before people take concrete steps to end an intimate partnership, they usually need time to mentally prepare themselves:

After realizing there was a problem, it took me a year to finally have the courage to step out. But it was a year of, "I don't want to be here anymore. Where do I want to be?" I didn't know. "I don't want this, but I'm not sure what I do want." It was hard. It wasn't overnight. It was a whole journey of shedding off these false self-images and picking up who I truly believe I am in my core. And I'm still doing that. In this new relationship, I have room to flourish, so I stay.

—JACOB

Self-understanding improves a person's self-concept and self-esteem thereby increasing their sense of inner strength and self-respect. In addition, because self-understanding reduces self-judgment, it also makes people less susceptible to judgment from others, removing a major obstacle on the road to recovery.

SUMMARY

- People often feel shame about being in an abusive relationship.

- Validation from empathic, supportive others reduces self-judgment and is a vital part of the healing process.

- Family of origin experiences often set the stage for people to accept abuse in their adult relationships.

- Vulnerabilities and faults don't cause the abuse.

- Addictions don't cause the abuse.

- Abuse has a severe detrimental effect on a person's mental and physical health.

- Because of the innate need to bond with a significant other, ending an intimate relationship is difficult, even when abuse is involved.

ACTIVITY

1. Are there ways in which you have judged yourself in the context of the abusive relationship? What is it you say to yourself? What, if anything, in this chapter has helped you feel less self-judgment?

2. Have you felt or feared judgment from people outside the relationship? Whose opinion has the most influence on you? After reading this book so far, do you think they understand emotional abuse enough to make a fair judgment?

3. Have you experienced understanding and validation from

people outside the relationship? Was that helpful to you? In what ways?

4. Can you look back on your family of origin experience and discern if you learned unhealthy patterns there that set the stage for you to accept abuse from an intimate partner? If so, what did you learn about yourself and relationships in general that prepared you to accept abuse?

5. Have you believed that your faults and vulnerabilities caused the abuse in your relationship? Are there ways in which your partner fostered and encouraged those beliefs? How?

6. Are there ways in which your partner magnified and/or exploited your vulnerabilities for their own advantage? How?

7. Are anxiety and depression becoming part of your mental health picture? What symptoms do you have? When did they start? Have they gotten worse over time? What support do you need?

8. Do you have physical ailments that doctors say are due to stress or anxiety? What are they? When did they start?

IS IT SUPPOSED TO BE THIS HARD?

No. The ongoing negative judgment that is part of emotional abuse saps the abused partner's life energy. By contrast, when people feel a safe and secure bond with their significant other, they have higher self-esteem, feel more empowered, more confident, more independent, and manage life's stressors better.[23] In addition, they enjoy better physical health outcomes than people in hostile and/or neglectful relationships.[24]

CHAPTER 10

THE PATH TO EMPOWERMENT

"I Am Honoring Me Today"

Toward the end of our relationship, it was really about finding myself. Then I left, and I was very frail. My soul was like Tinker Bell. Remember how you had to clap a lot to bring her back to life? So I had to put myself back together.

—SABRINA

Being out from under his negative cloud, I am seeing life more clearly now. I am more confident, independent, open-minded, willing to take risks, advocating for my needs, and asking for what I want. I have healthy boundaries now.

—SIERRA

Can you relate to how Sabrina felt at the end of her relationship? Like Tinker Bell who was starting to fade away and needed support and encouragement to bring her life energy back? Are you beginning to see through the negative cloud of emotional abuse? Can you imagine yourself feeling like Sierra did after she had been out of the relationship for a while? Are you ready to start that journey?

The road from abuse to healing and empowerment includes the following:

- Connecting with empathic, supportive others
- Recognizing that abuse has occurred
- Detaching from the abuser
- Setting boundaries
- Taking concrete steps to gain a sense of strength and autonomy

Like most of life, the path to empowerment is a process that rarely goes in a straight line. People learn new things, try to apply them, make mistakes, have self-doubts, get encouragement, try again, make more mistakes, learn from them, get more encouragement, take another step, etc:

> *When I was in that marriage, I had some friendships that were the best I could do at the time. But since then, I found that I was still tolerating a lot of crap in relationships. So, I have changed some of those friendships and incorporated other people who are healthier.*
>
> —JAYLA

> *I feel strong today. I know I am valuable today. I will not compromise how I think or feel, and I do know how to say what I want. I still acquiesce more than I should, though, so I'm still working on it.*
>
> —BELINDA

> *I have gotten back on the horse eight times after falling off seven. I am a badass! Having that narrative of resiliency, that feels like empowerment.*
>
> —ABIGAIL

It is okay, it's even expected, that people will get things wrong and make mistakes as they learn anything new. To expect otherwise is unrealistic. Breaking old patterns and creating new ways of being take time. That is why support from compassionate others and self-compassion are such valuable assets on this journey.

THE POWER OF POSITIVE SUPPORT

Getting support from caring others is essential to recovering from an abusive relationship. People who have been struggling with emotional abuse are usually mentally, emotionally, and physically exhausted. Their confidence is low, and their anxiety is high. They are disheartened by their failed efforts to create a loving relationship, and they often feel hopeless and alone. Just like Tinker Bell was revived when others were there for her, so abuse survivors are rejuvenated by consistent support and encouragement from compassionate others:

> *The first thing I had to do was stop trying to handle it on my own. I learned there is strength in numbers, and that my decisions weren't always the best. I needed to run things past someone else, or ask for advice, or to let them know I wasn't as strong as I looked and I needed help, too. I have different networks now that help me.*
>
> —BELINDA

Connecting with others who understand the situation and are willing to help is of the utmost importance, especially in the early stages of the healing process.

By definition, emotionally abused partners have been subjected to ongoing negative feedback about who they are, their innate qualities, skills, interests, and beliefs. When people recovering from abuse have others in their support system who see their positive aspects and express appreciation for who they are, what they do, and the efforts they make, they begin to believe in themselves:

> *I realized, even though it was just these few caseworkers, because I didn't have friends yet, that people liked me, and they believed in me, so then I started believing in myself a*

little bit. Then I realized that my dad was proud of me, and I started feeling really inspired.

—Chloe

Just as abused partners internalized the negative messages from the abuser, they begin to internalize positive messages from caring others. With time, the abused person relies less on outside messaging to maintain a healthy self-image:

> *I finally reached the point where I can recognize how I feel, and respect how I feel. I honor my feelings and allow myself to respond to what I need and take care of myself. That's all very empowering. I'm making good decisions now. And I recognize abuse. There was a time when the partner I'm with now was somewhat abusive, and I nipped it in the bud.*

—Jackie

As people believe in themselves more and start taking actions that support their wellness, they become more self-assured and feel more autonomous.

There are a variety of ways in which people recovering from abuse can get support. Most people report that individual therapy was invaluable to their recovery:

> *I wouldn't be the person I am today if I hadn't gone through therapy.*

—Anika

In addition to therapy, other sources of support include friends and family connections, a supportive church community, the Crisis Helpline, and groups such as Al-Anon, CoDA (Co-Dependents

Anonymous), and Adult Children of Alcoholics. Most communities have state and county mental health services for people of limited means. The crisis helpline can help locate additional resources in the local community. Please see the Recommended Resources section on page 297.

KNOWLEDGE IS POWER

To address a problem, a clear assessment of the issue is crucial. The problem in emotionally abusive relationships is not that abused partners didn't try hard enough or long enough, or were too selfish, or not smart enough, or just didn't do things the right way. The problem is they were with an abuser:

> *I tried everything. But that's not even the point. The point is you shouldn't have to. It's human nature that if you are in a relationship with someone you care about and there is a problem, you are going to want to fix it. But after a couple of different reasonable attempts to communicate, connect, discuss adult to adult, if it's not working, it's not going to work. There are not enough tips, tricks, and methods to get an abuser to stop abusing. The more we try, the more we're in a trap. And then you're in a trap that could last years.*
>
> —SAMANTHA

It is a bitter pill to swallow when someone realizes their significant other is an abuser, but it is often what sets them on the path to recovery.

Another part of recognizing the problem is taking stock of the cost to the abused partner. The mental and physical toll of emotional abuse is often the impetus for people to take the action necessary to save themselves. For many it even feels like a survival issue:

> *There were times when I was planning to commit suicide, but I was also having a repeated image of myself in an old church graveyard. There was a gate, and I could see that outside it there was open pastureland with woods beyond, but there were no signs. There were no trails. I had no idea where to go*

*if I walked through the gate, but I knew if I stayed I would
be part of that graveyard. That image showed me that my
spirit was dying even if I didn't kill my body. That's when I
decided he wasn't allowed to take my spiritual and mental
health. Then I got angry and felt my power rising.*

—TERRI

*Experiencing all that abuse he threw at me actually allowed
me to get in touch with myself on a deeper level than I've
ever known, because things were so bad that I had to find
survival inside of me. I had to care about myself because I
had no other choice.*

—SABRINA

Sometimes a physical health crisis is the wake-up call:

My turning point was after the stroke. I didn't want to die.

—DENISE

Other times clarity comes when abused partners see the cost of
the abuse to their children:

*I think most people will take it, but if you mess with my
kids…. At first I took it because I thought that staying was
the best thing for them. Then I left because I saw how it was
hurting them.*

—ANIKA

For many people, just getting a clear picture of the abuse and its
costs is empowering:

*I've been dealing with it for eight years, trying to make sense
of it. I could have left earlier, but I didn't. Now I understand*

what it's all about, how it all happened, and it makes me
feel like a stronger person.

—DENISE

The old saying, "knowledge is power" certainly applies to people who gain clarity after living with the confusion that is associated with emotional abuse.

Finally, a vital piece of information for people recovering from abuse is seeing how they contributed to the abusive situation by giving their power away:

The only thing I can take responsibility for in my life is that I
allowed it to happen. And that didn't make me bad or weak,
or whatever, it made me unaware. If I had more informa-
tion, if I had more self-confidence, I could have walked away
sooner. I allowed it to happen, and now I walk away. Now
I am in control.

—JACOB

Taking an honest look at how partners have forfeited their power in the relationship, primarily by failing to set boundaries, is a necessary step in claiming it back.

THE HEALING POWER OF ANGER

Once people realize they have been living with abuse, they often feel shocked, betrayed, ashamed, and then angry:

> *When I started realizing he was abusive, I was just so angry, angry, angry. Very angry.*
>
> —JACKIE

Anger is an appropriate response to a violation or injustice.

The goal of healthy anger is protection. It is a motivating force that has a role in self-care. However, anger is so often expressed with aggression and violence that its positive function gets lost, and people come to believe that anger itself is unacceptable.

Abused partners often learned early in life to deny their anger. They may have been taught that it is an unacceptable emotion:

> *My mother taught me that I was not allowed to get angry.*
>
> —JACKIE

Or the abused person may have come to believe anger was incompatible with their role as the compassionate caretaker in the family:

> *It was always, "I am not violent. I am not my mother. I am not angry. That's not who I am."*
>
> —PAOLA

One way people deny themselves power is by denying their anger. They become passive out of fear of perpetrating anger on others.

Another possibility is that the anger of adults in the home was so intimidating that the child was afraid to express their own anger:

*I didn't even know what the feeling of anger was because all
I ever experienced was anger projected at me. I didn't know
what my own anger felt like. It was almost as if because of
the abuser throwing so much toxic anger at me, I absolutely
defaulted into not being angry—I couldn't access it. You
know what is interesting? My friends would do the anger for
me, on my behalf, until I knew how to do the anger myself.
They made me realize that it was okay for me to get angry. I
literally had to be shown how to do it.*

—PAOLA

Suppressing the healthy expression of anger cuts off an important
avenue for self-protection and self-care:

*My ex reinforced exactly what my mother taught me, which
was that you are not allowed to get angry. So I was angry,
but I kept it underground so it fueled my phobias and panic
attacks and did a lot of damage. I felt bad about myself for
years. Then I went into therapy and realized that I needed
to get angry to be mentally stable and healthy.*

—JACKIE

While anger that is expressed aggressively is destructive, so is anger
that is habitually suppressed.

ANGER, MY FRIEND

Once abused people can't deny their anger any longer, they often
have an internal struggle trying to reconcile anger with their self-
image as a kind, loving person. Terri shared a journal entry about the
psycho-spiritual identity crisis her anger engendered:

Anger, My Friend. It is my anger that gave me power. When I finally stopped trying to quell my anger—when it got too strong for me to quell anymore, it became a productive force because it spurred me to respond to the circumstances that created the anger in the first place. When I allowed it to work, it made me strong enough to set parameters and change my circumstances.

One of the things I've been asking myself is, "Why did I stay?" Part of the answer is that I would not be instructed by my anger. Rather than see it as a sign, a friend with advice to give, I saw it as an evil to overcome.

Being angry, living with it, walking with it, responding to it, at first seemed very, very wrong, but alas, I had no choice because it had grown much, much stronger than I. I had to drop all my attempts at being loving and forgiving and depend on the mercy of God. I had to admit that I was no spiritual master. I was not nearly virtuous or heroic enough to over-come the anger I felt. I went with this anger because I believed to do otherwise would be to allow myself to be destroyed. I had to do what I had to do to save myself. And now I real-ize that Anger, My Friend, has initiated the changes to the situation that gave rise to the anger to begin with.

Healthy anger is a profound act of self-love that honors the sanctity and integrity of the self enough to protect it against the degradation inherent in abuse.

Sometimes, when people who have been passive in the face of abuse finally allow themselves to feel and act on their anger, they let the pendulum swing too far into aggression:

I didn't know how to be appropriately angry. So when I finally became angry, the rage was over the top. It was like

all the experiences of anger that had been suppressed became
this blinding rage, which was inappropriate.

—PAOLA

For those who self-identify as empathic, compassionate, loving people, acting out with aggressive anger feels contrary to their nature:

I don't want to become the person who has to rage and shout and
overpower people. That doesn't feel good to me. My mother was
a shouter, a rager. I was afraid that it would become a habit.

—SAMANTHA

Part of healing from abuse is learning how to be true to that core identity of being a compassionate person while still honoring the self-protective force of healthy anger. When people know how to do that, they have become compassionate warriors.

BECOMING A COMPASSIONATE WARRIOR

Compassionate warriors are people who have learned to balance the force of healthy anger with their desire to be kind individuals.

- Compassionate warriors use protective anger to detach from the abuser without the need to demean, diminish, or punish them.

- Compassionate warriors use the motivating force of healthy anger to change themselves without expecting change from the abuser.

- Compassionate warriors use protective anger to fortify their boundaries and hold them with conviction. Their goal is to reclaim their power without disempowering another, although abusers will object to losing their abusive power and control.

- Compassionate warriors use healthy anger to hold abusers accountable for their actions. They do not compromise their boundaries because the abuser doesn't like them.

- Compassionate warriors use the motivating force of healthy anger to propel them forward as they step away from abuse and toward their own safety, health, and growth.

- Compassionate warriors are self-forgiving when they fail to hold boundaries as firmly as they want or when they overstep by acting more aggressively than they would like. They apologize if necessary, regroup, and move on with resolve to do better next time.

While compassionate warriors initially use anger to feel strong, they don't need anger to stay strong. Compassionate warriors eventually feel empowered enough that their anger is relegated to its rightful function as an alert that a boundary is being violated and they need to take self-protective action, whether that means verbal expression to enforce the boundary, removing themselves from a situation, or taking any other healthy actions they need to take.

THERE IS POWER IN DETACHING

There are certain steps on the road to recovery that may elicit resistance from abused people. One of them is detaching from the abuser. Related to that is the importance of shifting their focus away from the abuser and onto their own need for self-care and healing. In addition, it is imperative that partners are aware of the risks inherent in setting boundaries or leaving an abuser. Throughout the remainder of this chapter there are "Alerts" that address each one of these issues.

ALERT #1: DETACHING

Just the word "detaching" may trigger anxiety, fear, and resistance in people who are experiencing traumatic bonding or who are just not ready to end the relationship yet. Part of healing from abuse is learning to respect yourself and insisting that others do so as well. It is not only okay, but essential, that you honor your own process. If the thought of detaching is distressful to you, continue going to therapy and being with supportive people as often as possible. Allow yourself to progress at your own pace.

Detaching is giving up expectations. In healthy relationships, expectations take the form of trust. Loving partners learn that they can trust each other to engage in respectful and considerate ways. They can count on each other to be there when one of them reaches out to connect on an emotional level. They can confidently rely on their partner to communicate, cooperate, and problem solve with them.

Emotional abusers derive a lot of their control in the relationship by manipulating their partner's hope for that kind of connection.

People recovering from abuse begin to claim their power when they detach from the idea that their significant other is willing or able to join them in any consistent effort to create a mutually respectful, considerate relationship:

> *I don't think he is a terrible person. I think he is troubled and doesn't know how to be a good partner. He is not capable of being a good partner.*
>
> —HALLIE

When emotionally abused people shift their energy and attention away from the expectation that their partner will change and that the relationship will become what they had hoped it would be, they can begin to invest their efforts in recovering from the abuse.

ALERT #2: FOCUSING ON SELF

The shift in focus from other to self can be a difficult step for emotionally abused partners because it goes against their tendency to focus on the needs of others and be compassionate toward them. It may help people recovering from abuse to remember that abusers tend to interpret their expressions of compassion and understanding as acceptance of the abuse and permission to continue abusing. So, in the context of an abusive relationship, compassion and understanding become enabling. Pema Chödrön (2001), a Buddhist monk and teacher, describes something called idiot compassion:

"This is when we avoid conflict and protect our good image by being kind when we should say a definite 'no.' Compassion doesn't imply only trying to be good. When we find ourselves in an aggressive relationship, we need to set clear boundaries. The kindest thing we can do for everyone concerned is to know when to say 'enough.'" (78-79)

Abuse violates the soul of the abuser as well as the abused, so taking steps to stop it is ultimately an act of compassion for both partners.

DETACHMENT IS FREEING

As people who have been abused detach from different aspects of the abusive relationship, they are freed up to tend to their own healing and growth.

Free to Begin Healing

When partners detach from the idea that they can love the abuser better, or heal them, they are freed up to focus on appropriate self-love and self-compassion:

> *Part of what kept me in it was the belief that I was powerful enough, strong enough, smart enough, compassionate enough, kind enough to change somebody. The truth is the only person I can change is me, and the only person that can change you is you. It's up to everybody to change themselves.*
>
> —SAMANTHA

While couples can create a loving, supportive environment for each other, every adult is responsible for their own internal journey. When people recovering from abuse focus on creating a healing environment for themselves through therapy, a support group, and/or a circle of supportive family and friends, they can go deeper on their own healing journey, learn more about how their strengths and weaknesses have shaped their lives, and discover what changes will enhance their growth and wellness.

Free to Create a Positive Identity

When partners detach from the abuser's negative feedback and opinions of them, they are freed up to focus on creating a more positive self-image:

> I don't have to do this anymore. I feel like I can finally go forward. I can change. I can get past this. I am not just a bunch of flaws, failures, and screwups. And actually, all this stuff I've been told I am terrible at, I'm really pretty good at! And it is just an overwhelming world of possibilities. Like when you throw open the curtains in the morning and the light hurts your eyes, but wow, the whole day is out in front of you.
>
> —VINCENT

A caring support system is an important part of the healing process precisely because abusers habitually reflect a distorted image back to their partner. Recognizing that distortion for what it is helps people make a more realistic assessment of both themselves and the abuser. Partners can begin to experience their strengths and positive qualities with more clarity and assurance.

Free to Find a Way Forward

When emotionally abused people detach from the need to figure out what is going on with the abuser, they are freed up to figure out what is really going on in the relationship:

> I was in therapy. I was just trying to survive. But I was also

*trying to figure him out. Always trying to figure out, what
do I do with him? How do I handle him? I worked really
hard trying to figure it all out.*

—Jackie

The relationship finally makes sense when the abused partner rec-
ognizes that they couldn't figure things out because the person they
loved and trusted was using manipulation, gaslighting, denial, and
power plays against them. Then they can shift their focus to figuring out how to get themselves into a safer situation:

*When I decided to leave him, I had to trust my inner voice
to help guide me through this, to figure out when and how to
leave, and to value myself enough to have the bravery to do it.*

—Sabrina

Whether the partner is ready to leave immediately or not, they
can put their attention on figuring out their next steps instead of trying to figure out the abuser.

Free from Abuse

Finally, when partners detach from the positive times with an
abuser, they are freed up to see how the relationship is harming them:

*At some point I realized the cost of the good times was just too
high. There was too much that wasn't being fulfilled and too
much that was damaging to justify the really good moments.*

—Hallie

Recognizing how damaging the relationship has been can help
partners resist the impulse to return to the abuser:

For me, it took being physically separated from my ex and

being around normal, healthy relationships to really put that
unhealthy relationship in perspective. Then when something
crazy or dramatic happened, it felt crazier and more dra-
matic, as it should have. I could see it better because I was
in a normal space in the rest of my life.

—HALLIE

People recovering from abuse need to detach from the good times as well as the hurtful times; otherwise, the abuser will retain the power to draw them back into the abuse. When partners are able to recognize that the positive times are actually part of the abuse process, they are free to create a new life where abuse is not the cost of love.

DETACHING FROM REACTIVE FEELINGS

"Don't take it personally." That may sound like off-the-cuff advice that doesn't make sense in an abusive situation, because when a person has been subjected to repeated verbal and emotional assaults by their most trusted intimate other for months, years, or decades, the abuse surely *feels* personal.

But the truth is that the abuse was always about the abuser's own psychological issues, never about what their partner did or didn't do. The partner was unwittingly cast as an actor in the abuser's internal drama. When people recovering from abuse see how they have been playing their part, they can recast themselves in a more empowered role. A detached partner can look at the abuser's toxic behavior and say, "There they are doing that thing again. I don't have to buy into that scenario. I can choose a different role. I can even walk off the stage."

It is the abused person's attachment to their significant other and their hope of creating a healthy relationship the makes them vulnerable to emotional abuse. As partners detach, the abuser's ability to elicit reactions like hurt, anxiety, confusion, and shame is diminished considerably, so partners become less emotionally vulnerable and, consequently, less emotionally reactive. The abuser's power to cause harm decreases, and the partner's sense of safety and empowerment increases.

CLAIMING POWER
THROUGH BOUNDARIES

Boundaries are limits. People who have good boundaries are clear about what their limits are. They are able to let others know what they are and are not willing to do, and what treatment they will and will not accept. Knowledge, support, protective anger, and detaching all help people recovering from abuse to set boundaries effectively.

Knowledge

For instance, recognizing the abuse for what it is and how harmful it has been helps people see why it is necessary to set boundaries:

> *Now that I'm aware of it I can look at it and say, "I know exactly what you are doing here, and it's not going to work today." But then I wasn't so cognizant of it.*
>
> —ALEC

When people see clearly how they have been manipulated or hurt by the abuser, they become more firm and consistent in setting boundaries.

Support

A positive support system helps people who have been abused believe that they are worthy of protecting themselves:

> *It all comes down to I'd never put up boundaries. It took me so many years to say, "I'm done. These are my boundaries. Don't cross my boundaries." Why didn't I put up boundaries before? Because I didn't think I was worthy enough. So the empowerment part is realizing that even if I'm alone, I'm worth it. And I want other people to realize that I'm worth it.*
>
> —DENISE

Protective Anger

As people build self-esteem, they are more inclined to see the abuses for what they are—violations of the self. Consequently, they are better prepared to defend themselves when the need arises:

> *When you start to build up your self-esteem from the core out, you get angry that someone thinks they can treat you like that.*
>
> —ANIKA

As people get better at setting boundaries, they experience their own strength, increase their self-respect, and develop an internal sense of empowerment.

Detachment

Finally, detachment helps partners reduce their emotional reactivity to the abuser's manipulations and degradations:

> *In the beginning it was, "Oh, why are you saying that? That is so hurtful." I was shocked. I had very emotional responses. I wanted to talk it through. I wanted to fix it. Then over time I just started to walk away from it, disengage. As I read more and learned more, I finally got to, "I'm not taking this anymore, and you're not talking to me like that anymore." Then you just disengage.*
>
> —ANIKA

People can think more clearly, make more rational decisions, and take more effective action when they are not in a highly emotional state.

BOUNDARIES CHANGE THE
RELATIONSHIP CONTRACT

Setting boundaries is a way for people who are overcoming abuse to claim more power in a relationship that has been characterized by a drastic imbalance of power. It changes the relationship contract *whether the abuser chooses to cooperate or not.*

Unlike the demeaning, destructive use of power in abuse, the power involved in boundary setting is protective. It doesn't aim to harm the other person, but it doesn't aim to save them from feeling hurt or disappointment when they don't get their way, either:

> *For most of the marriage, I was intimidated by his anger. I tried to do things to avoid it, to fix things before he would get angry about them. Then at some point I decided, "You know what? It's okay if he's angry." For years I let his anger pull my strings and keep me boxed in. I'm not doing that anymore. He can get angry and yell all he wants to. I'm not reacting to that anymore.*
>
> —TERRI

Nor does the partner try to save the abuser from the consequences of their actions:

> *A lot of times people will say, "Oh, hurt people hurt people." No. I don't care if they were abused, I don't care. They are grown up. They have access to mental health, doctors, and therapists. If they're hurting people, that's bad. It doesn't matter what happened in the past. They are 100% responsible for their behavior.*
>
> —SAMANTHA

> *It doesn't matter what your mother did to you when you were six. You're not allowed to treat me like that today.*
>
> —TERRI

Instead of making allowances in the name of compassion, boundary setting holds people accountable for their behaviors. As long as someone is in relationship with an abuser, there will be ongoing power struggles, but setting boundaries helps people claim more power more of the time.

ALERT #3: PUSHBACK FROM THE ABUSER

It is important for partners setting boundaries with an abuser to be aware that they won't give up power and control easily. The abusive behaviors may become more extreme. Abusers often try to intimidate or manipulate the partner back into the old relationship contract. Abusers are likely to ignore or challenge any boundaries on their controlling behaviors. They may experience the boundaries as unfair and even abusive toward them and accuse the partner of being the true abuser.

There is a danger that emotional abuse will escalate to physical abuse. It is important for abused people to assess the risk and proceed with safety and self-care in mind. It is not always prudent or safe to set healthy boundaries with an unhealthy individual.

The Domestic Violence Hotline (page 297) can help you assess your dangers and learn ways to take protective actions.

THE CENTRAL QUESTION
IN SETTING BOUNDARIES

Throughut the course of an emotionally abusive relationship, many abused people do stand up to the abuser, however their goal is usually to convince the abuser to stop the abusive behavior. That, of course, is a reasonable request, but it leaves the power in the abuser's hands; they can choose to change or not, and they usually do not. Consequently, the partner is left feeling frustrated and disempowered.

The central question in setting boundaries is not, "How can I get my partner to change?" but, "How do I claim my power in this situation?" Another way to think about it is, "How do I keep the ball in my court?"

Boundaries When The Relationship Is Ending

For example, people who are exiting the relationship can keep the ball in their court by ending or minimizing contact with an ex who continues to be abusive. Blocking their number and unfriending them on social media are some options. If communication is necessary during the separation/divorce process, partners can insist that all contact go through the lawyers.

A restraining order may be advisable if the ex escalates to harassing, stalking, or other threatening behaviors; partners will need to check the laws about this in their area. If the abuse has become physically violent, it may be necessary to move to a safe house or other secure location. The Domestic Violence Hotline provides information to help with these steps.

Boundaries When There Are Children

When children are involved, abusers may use necessary communication to provoke, harass, or intimidate their ex partner. Creating an email account exclusively for conducting business regarding the children is one way to set boundaries on abusive communication.

That way, partners can engage on their own terms rather than allowing the abuser to intrude on their daily activities and communication channels. If the abuser ignores this request and continues to initiate communication in other ways, the partner can respond with, "I see you emailed me at _____ (or called or texted). I will only respond to communications left at abc@respectmyboundaries.com. Please contact me there. Thank you."

Simply ignoring any unnecessary or inappropriate communication is also effective.

If communications continue to be laced with abuse that triggers the partner, they might consider enlisting an ally to review emails and other forms of written communication from the abuser until they stop, or the partner is no longer upset by them.

In addition, partners can put boundaries around in-person contact when the abuser uses that opportunity to bait or undermine them. For instance, exchanging the children in public places or having someone with them can be helpful. Another way to avoid taking the bait is to imagine the encounter will appear on social media or be viewed in a courtroom (as, indeed, it may). People tend to be on their best behavior when there are witnesses.

Partners know the abuser's favorite tactics. Thinking ahead about the question, "How can I keep my power in this situation?" will help them strategize in advance. For example, partners with shared custody can't make their ex pick up or drop off the children on time, but they can make contingency plans when timing is important. If the partner is planning on going away for the weekend or to an important work or social meeting and needs to leave at a specific time, they can arrange to have the children picked up at a family member's or friend's house.

There will, no doubt, be times when the partner isn't on top of things and gets taken in. From there, they can forgive themselves, shake it off, and learn from it so they can make a more effective plan the next time, always asking themselves, "How do I keep my power?"

Boundaries When The Relationship Continues

Sometimes people need to stay in the relationship while they lay the groundwork necessary to make a safe and secure exit, for instance finding a safe place to stay, finishing their education, or procuring a suitable job. Some people may choose to stay indefinitely because they think it is best for the children, or for financial/medical reasons:

> *We had an adopted son, and I wanted to provide him with*
> *as much stability as I could, considering his adoption issues.*
> *And there were also financial and healthcare considerations.*
> *I needed to be on a group plan. I wouldn't have been able to*
> *afford insurance because I had pre-existing conditions.*
>
> —JAYLA

In these cases, setting boundaries will be an ongoing practice. One of the most effective ways to maintain power in a continuing relationship is to become a master of the "I statement." This communication technique also serves partners well in other areas of life, including future relationships.

BECOMING A MASTER OF THE "I STATEMENT"

Abuse undermines a person's sense of self. Each "I statement" a person who is overcoming abuse makes is a reminder to themselves and others that they are asserting their selfhood and claiming their power. The best way to project a sense of empowerment when making "I statements" is to use a clear, neutral tone of voice, direct eye contact, a confident posture, and an attitude that says, "I mean what I say." Of course, it is important to follow through with action when boundaries are ignored. That usually means exiting the abusive situation.

Below are some examples of "I statements." They are just that, examples. Finding your own words and practicing by saying them out loud, even in front of a mirror, can be very helpful. Role-playing with an ally is another good way to increase confidence.

I Statements for Different Situations

A classic "I feel" statement has three parts:

> *I feel* _____
>
> *When* _____,
>
> *And I would like* _____.

For example, "I feel hurt when you call me names, and I would like you to be more respectful of me." That formula is effective when the speaker has reason to believe the other person: (a) cares how they feel, (b) is willing to listen to their complaint, and (c) is inclined to cooperate with their request for change or negotiate another mutually agreeable solution. In the unlikely event that an emotionally abused person has not already used this approach, it is worth a try. However, most abused people have already spent a great deal of time sharing their feelings, explaining why the abusive behavior is hurtful, and asking for a change, all to no avail.

Using I Statements to Inform

A classic "I feel statement" asks the other person to change their behavior. By using "I statements" to inform rather than request, partners hold on to their power. They don't depend on change from the abuser. They simply declare their limits and what they will do to hold them:

> *"If you continue to call me names, I'm going to leave the room."*

This statement should not be repeated. This is not the time for second chances. It is of the utmost importance that people consistently and immediately follow through with their chosen course of action—or they forfeit their power, and the abuse will continue and likely escalate. It can be helpful to spend that time away talking to a supportive person, exercising, or doing some other enjoyable activity that will restore equilibrium and positive energy.

Using I Statements to De-Escalate

Here is an example of using an "I statement" to inform when the abuser is becoming angry and beginning to yell:

> *"I won't engage with someone who is yelling at me. If you stop, we can talk. Otherwise, I'm leaving."*

Tip: It is not effective to tell an aggravated person to calm down or take a time out. It rarely calms them down, and it usually escalates the situation. A more de-escalating response would be:

> *"I shut down (or get triggered) when people yell at me. I'm going to take a timeout. We can try to talk about this later if you still want to."*

By claiming the need for a timeout for themselves, whether they really need one or not, the partner creates a timeout for the abuser, too. Stating it this way both empowers the partner and avoids triggering the abuser to get offensively defensive. Much of emotional abuse is opportunistic. There is a good chance the timeout will take the energy out of that particular abusive incident. Unless you feel that there was some real merit in what they were yelling about, don't initiate a return to the topic. If the abuser had a legitimate complaint, they will bring it up again, and if they do so in a respectful way, that's the time to respond.

Using I Statements In the Face of Gaslighting

Gaslighting often happens unexpectedly and is disorienting. It can be difficult to find an effective response in those conditions. Partners can make an "I statement" that identifies and owns the confusion, such as:

> *"I'm not sure what is going on right now. I need to take a step back and clear my head."*

Again, don't initiate a return to the topic. Partners can use their timeout to make a call to someone in their support group for a reality check and emotional support if the gaslighting has left them confused, frustrated, or feeling off balance.

Using I Statements To Fend Off Manipulation

There is very little abusers can't twist around to use against their partners. When a person senses they are being manipulated, they can use an "I statement" to disengage:

> *"I'm not sure what's going on right now, but it doesn't feel good to me. I need to step away from this situation for a while."*

People can use the time away to sort out the manipulation and make a more clear-headed decision about how they want to respond. If appropriate, they can follow up with another kind of "I statement" that allows them to assert their boundaries while still being considerate of the other. For instance:

> *"I am willing to do this, but not that."*

Taking a timeout gives a person the chance to think about various ways they can keep their power.

Using I Statements with Consideration

Setting boundaries doesn't mean partners can't be considerate, especially when there is not a conflict. For instance, they can acknowledge the abuser's feelings and still go forward with their plans:

> *"I know you don't like it when I go out with my friends, but it is important to me to spend some time hanging out with them. We'll be at _____. I expect to be home by _____. I'll text you if that changes."*

While being considerate, partners need to be cautious about getting drawn into long explanations about why they are doing what they are doing or defending the need to do it. Abusers are likely to turn explanations into a manipulative debate that will distract the partner from their goal and sap their power. One way to avoid getting pulled into an abuser's manipulations is an old Alcoholics Anonymous trope: KISS. Keep It Simple, Stupid. The more streamlined the statement, the less ammunition the abuser has.

In addition, people overcoming abuse will need to put firm boundaries around their own reactions to the abuser's acts of kindness. They can politely express appreciation for thoughtfulness while staying detached from the idea that it means the abuser has changed and the relationship is improving. It is important to take niceties at face value. A mental reminder such as: "This is a pleasant encounter for this moment, but it can turn into abuse at any time" can help partners keep their perspective.

To be clear, the purpose is to be courteous, not to make an emotional connection with the abuser. As soon as partners start hoping for a loving relationship with the abuser, they make themselves vulnerable to abuse again. Staying detached from the expectation of a healthy partnership makes it much easier to set and hold boundaries.

And because holding boundaries once they are set is so important, people should be careful to only set boundaries that they can reasonably expect to keep. For instance, if the couple is arguing while driving down the highway at 70 miles per hour and the abused partner says they will get out of the car if the abuser doesn't stop yelling, they have set a boundary they can't enforce.

Sometimes the answer to, "How can I keep my power in this situation?" is, "I can't." The answer then is to emotionally and/or physically detach from the situation as much as possible and then engage in self-care at the first opportunity. Planning ahead about ways to avoid those "no power" situations can increase a sense of empowerment in both emotional and practical ways.

Boundary setting may not always work. Abusers are skilled at setting up power-over situations and partners are likely to get caught up in them at times. But just the act of speaking up and setting boundaries increases a sense of empowerment and self-respect.

A Guide To "I Statements" In Emotional Abuse

In This Situation:	Use a Statement Like This:
To inform (not request), use this:	*"If you continue to call me names, I'm going to leave the room."*
To de-escalate when partner is angry/yelling, use this:	*"I won't engage with someone who is yelling at me. If you stop, we can talk. Otherwise, I'm leaving."* OR *"I shut down (or get triggered) when people yell at me. I'm going to take a timeout. We can try to talk about this later if you still want to."*
If partner is gaslighting you, use this:	*"I'm not sure what is going on right now. I need to take a step back and clear my head."*
If partner is trying to manipulate you, use this:	*"I'm not sure what's going on right now, but it doesn't feel good to me. I need to step away from this situation for a while."* AND/OR *"I am willing to do this, but not that."*
To show that you are considering their feelings, while setting a boundary with an I statement, say something like this:	*"I know you don't like it when I go out with my friends (or do other things), but it is important to me to spend some time hanging out with them (have my other need met). We'll be at _____. I expect to be home by _____. I'll text you if that changes."*

TAKING ACTION STEPS IS EMPOWERING

Another way to increase empowerment is to take action steps. What kind of action steps will depend on where a person is on their path to recovery. Many people will be ready to call a lawyer or pack up their things shortly after realizing that the relationship is abusive. Others may need time to lay the groundwork necessary for a safe exit, taking into account their physical and financial wellbeing. Some will need to start small and begin building their support system, strength, and self-confidence slowly.

One person described being so depressed that microwaving a potato felt like an accomplishment she was proud of. She was energized enough by that small step to take other steps. Since she enjoyed the taste of food, she was inspired to brush her teeth, then that motivated her to take better care of other aspects of her hygiene. Finally, when she felt less ashamed of herself, she started reaching out to family members. By taking small steps, then bigger and bigger steps, she eventually gained the confidence she needed to end the relationship.

THE STEPS TO EMPOWERMENT BUILD ON EACH OTHER

Each action step, no matter how small, builds self-esteem and helps the person moving on from abuse to take the next step with a little more self-assurance. For instance, learning about abuse and reaching out to others for support are early steps on the way to empowerment. Those steps make it easier to detach and set boundaries. Each boundary set and kept reinforces self-worth and inner strength.

Now let's look at other concrete action steps that can help on the path to empowerment.

Tending To Self-Care:

> *I am even more intent about nutrition and taking care of my body now.*
>
> —JAYLA

> *I started a regular fitness program. As I got stronger in my body, I started to feel stronger mentally and emotionally. I wasn't so beaten down. I started to feel like a strong person.*
>
> —TERRI

> *I would feel the anxiety building, and I would say, "Okay, get on your shoes and get out the door." I knew that I had to keep moving my body, so I literally would walk miles a day, and that was helpful. Sometimes I would talk to people on my phone while I was walking.*
>
> —PORCHIA

Self-soothing techniques are another aspect of self-care that help people calm themselves when they are upset. Some examples are positive self-talk, deep breathing and muscle relaxation, meditation, or a spiritual practice. Therapists and support groups can help personalize self-soothing techniques so they are more effective. Here are some self-soothers to try:

- The 4-4-8 Breath. Inhale to a count of 4. Hold for 4. Exhale for 8. This is a form of Mindfulness-Based Stress Reduction.

- Breathe in "peace." Breathe out "release" of whatever stress, fear, or negative thoughts or energy you need to let go of.

- Try very gentle yoga, qi gong (chi gong), or tai chi. Almost anyone, in any physical condition, can do these moving meditations, which have been proven to improve health and restore a sense of peace and well-being.

- Get outside. Nature nurtures. Turn off notifications if you can and just focus on the sounds of the birds, the leaves swaying in the breeze, the sun or moon or starlight.

Finding A Creative Outlet:

I wrote a lot of poetry, so I was able to express my pain and angst that way. And I would sing and dance. It was my relationship with my best friend and my artwork that saved me.

—PAOLA

Sometimes people have lost sight of, or never had the chance to explore, creative endeavors. Searching for areas of interest is, itself, an action step and a process of self-discovery. There is no end to online videos that introduce people to creative outlets they can explore. Trying different creative arts, learning a musical instrument, joining a singing group or even a local theater or improv group or are just a few ideas of how to expand, express, and empower yourself on this journey to greater happiness and fulfillment.

Starting A Hobby Or An Interest Outside The Home:

Joining an adult sports team is one example. Taking online or in-person classes to learn new skills such as woodworking, gardening, cooking, or do-it-yourself projects are other possibilities. Getting more involved in your spiritual community or volunteering for a cause you believe in are other possible ways to boost your happiness and autonomy bit by bit. Discovering new interests outside the relationship can help you see yourself in new, more positive ways:

I have become more aware of what I like to do, and I am pursuing it. I started to do volunteer ushering. I am very creative. I am pursuing my creative interests. I'm taking adult education programs.

—JAYLA

I did self-development by reading books and attending workshops.

—SIERRA

I stay empowered by helping others. I went to school to become a Certified Addictions Counselor. Even at the age of 60, I am doing things to better myself.

—BELINDA

It is helpful to have goals. If long-term goals are too much to think about, daily goals are a good start: "What is one small thing I can do today to help me feel stronger, surer, and more empowered?"

As people gain confidence, they feel more able to take bigger steps such as learning to drive, getting a job or job training, and going back to school. Paige, a recent immigrant, explains how school helped beyond the education she was getting:

When I started school, my English was not that good, so I just took one class that first semester, because I didn't know how hard it was going to be to understand. The day he left the house, I was devastated, and what did I do? I went to study. I studied more than I ever did in my life, and I got a 104 on my test. So that gave me more confidence to finish school. And I also started to get to know more people and get more support out of it. I think the support was very important.

Acting on behalf of their own mental, emotional, and physical health helps people moving on from abuse bolster their sense of strength and empowerment. While connecting with caring and supportive others is a crucial part of a general mental health picture, as people experience their own strength through action steps, they are less dependent on external messages to feel their self-worth.

PREPARING TO LEAVE

Once partners decide to end the relationship, their actions steps will include making concrete plans on how to best achieve that goal.

ALERT # 4 ASSESS YOUR RISKS

Abused people are most at risk of an escalation in abuse when they are leaving the relationship. There is a risk that emotional abuse will turn into physical abuse, or that the abuser will take other serious retaliatory actions. It is important for abused people to assess the risks to themselves and their loved ones when they consider when and how to best exit an abusive relationship. The Domestic Violence Hotline is a good starting place to form a safe exit strategy for people who believe they are at risk. Please see the Recommended Resources section on page 297.

It is wise for people who are married, have children with their ex, or have other legal entanglements such as co-owning a home or a business to hire the best lawyer they can afford. Divorce settlements have long-lasting ramifications, and it is a lawyer's job to look out for their client's best interests.

Some people who left abusive relationships share their experiences:

You can't tell anybody when to leave. No matter how much you try. They'll know it. Once you make that decision, front load all the kinds of help you can. Don't do it alone. Don't feel that you're weak. You're not the only one who has gone through it.

—DENISE

Make an escape plan. Even if you're not getting beat up. Have a getaway bag stashed somewhere. It does feel good to have that bag. And you get empowered.

—SAMANTHA

Leaving him really built my self-confidence: the process of relying on myself, the process of getting a plan together to leave, and executing that plan. I read about other women's plans to leave online and talked to advocates on the hotline. I thought about leaving for months beforehand. And it was really empowering, even though it was scary. It felt morally wrong to deceive somebody for months, but I wasn't going to let him know that. I told myself: "No. I'm not deceiving somebody. I am looking out for myself and waiting for the right moment." The right moment for me was one where I wasn't tempted emotionally to take him back, where I knew I was safe, and I could get away and stay away. It was about emotional and physical safety.

—SABRINA

I got my finances straight. I acted like I was going to work out and looked for housing instead. If I had to lie, I did lie. I signed all the paperwork and then started packing.

—PAOLA

My parents ended up coming to help me move out. They hired movers. We didn't know if he would physically retaliate, so they made sure to stay with me during the move.

—SIERRA

Feeling empowered does not necessarily come from achieving all that was hoped for or doing things perfectly. Simply taking the action is self-confirming:

> *I felt strong when I went toe-to-toe with him in the divorce. I got the best attorney I could, and I didn't back down. I didn't ask for everything I deserved. I should have asked for more money and gone after what was right. I didn't get nearly that amount, but it was the fact that I did it. I didn't have family. I did it myself. He had his dad. He had attorneys, he had this and that. It was me, and of course my girlfriends in the background saying, "You've got this." I got full custody, and to me that was empowering.*
>
> —DENISE

Whether a person is ready to leave the relationship or feels the need to stay for a period of time, empathic support, information, appropriate self-care, detachment, boundaries, and action steps all contribute to an increased sense of strength, well-being, and self-reliance.

SUMMARY

- Supportive others are an important aid in recovering from abuse.

- Understanding what emotional abuse is and what its detrimental effects are helps people recovering from abuse to make a more accurate assessment of their relationship.

- Healthy anger has a protective function. It is a motivating force that helps people stand up for themselves without aiming to harm others.

- Detaching from the abuser and the expectation of a healthy relationship empowers people recovering from abuse because it reduces their emotional vulnerability. The more the partner detaches, the less power the abuser has over them.

- Boundaries are a way for people overcoming abuse to claim their own power and self-respect.

- As people moving on from abuse take action steps on behalf of their growth and wellness, they build their confidence and self-esteem.

- Abusers often escalate the abuse when their partners are leaving the relationship; including becoming physically violent. It is important for partners to assess their level of risk and plan accordingly.

ACTIVITY

1. Look back at your notes, comments, or journals for Chapters 1 through 6 to help you identify if your relationship is abusive. Whenever you feel unsure if you are experiencing abuse, refer to that list.

2. Make a list of the emotional, mental, spiritual, energetic, and physical costs of your relationship. When you wonder if you have the right to set boundaries or leave the relationship, refer to that list.

3. Are there ways you can envision using healthy, protective anger to increase your level of self-care without being punitive or retaliatory toward the abuser? What are they? Engage with your therapist or support group to learn additional ways.

4. Has knowledge about abuse and healthy anger motivated you to detach from the abuser and the hope of a better relationship? If so, in what ways have you been able to detach? Are there other areas where you are still working on detaching? What are they?

5. If you have not been able to detach, are you willing to explore your reluctance with a therapist or support group who will honor your process?

6. What are some situations where you could use "I statements" to set boundaries with the abuser? Think about what you might say and practice the words out loud. Feel free to choose words you are comfortable with and are relevant to your situation. If possible, role play with an ally.

7. Think about recurring abusive situations in your relationship. Ask yourself, "How can I keep my power in that situation? How do I keep the ball in my court?" Check with people in your support system to see if they have any suggestions.

8. What are some self-empowering steps you have already taken, no matter how small? How did you feel afterwards? Do you have an idea of what your next steps will be? What is something you can do today? Tomorrow? This week? This month? Are you ready to make mid-range and long-term goals? What might they be?

9. Do you have a support system you can rely on if you decide to leave your partner? Who are they? How would you contact them? How could they best help you?

IS IT SUPPOSED TO BE THIS HARD?

Well, yes. It is hard.

- The shocking realization that you've been abused is hard.

- Reaching out to others when you are afraid or ashamed is hard.

- Detaching from what you hoped for in the relationship is hard.

- Setting and holding boundaries is hard.

- Taking the risk to step out and try new things is hard.

- Ending a relationship is hard.

It's all hard, but you are not alone. People who have worked through those difficulties have some words of encouragement to offer you:

"You don't deserve this." For me that was the beginning. If I'm going to practice unconditional love, it has to include me. Choose those things that make you feel better about yourself.

—JACOB

I look different now than I did then. I look so much younger now. I act younger. There was such a seriousness about me. That was not me. My parents said my whole personality changed. Thank goodness I'm getting my personality back. I feel damaged a lot. I am still getting me back.

—SIERRA

I am taking care of me today. If I am not okay, I can't possibly have a successful relationship, so that is where I'm coming from at present.

—BELINDA

If you feel like nothing else can be better, that you can't find better, or there can't be a better situation, if you're just compromising because of that, know that it's a lie. Things CAN be better.

Leaving, I felt free. I felt empowered that he didn't know where I was. He couldn't make those decisions for me anymore. I could make my own decisions. I have a voice to do what I feel is right.

And I learned that I am resilient. I can come back from things. And I deserve really good things in life.

BECCA

It is my hope that this book has given you a better understanding of the difference between emotional abuse and the hard work of relationship so you can make more informed, empowered decisions about how to take appropriate, loving care of yourself. I also hope that the words of fellow travelers on the road from abuse to empowerment have inspired and encouraged you, and that you, like Becca, have learned that you are resilient, you can come back from these things, and you deserve really good things in life.

A NOTE TO HETEROSEXUAL MEN

Like other emotionally abused people, heterosexual men in abusive partnerships usually believe they are just doing the hard work of relationship, and their desire to be a caring and considerate partner is used against them. While news about women being abused by their male partners happens with distressing frequency, people rarely hear about men being abused by female partners, so when it happens to a man, he not only feels the shame of being an abused partner, as other abused people do, but he deals with an additional stigma:

> *For a long time, I was totally confused. I felt alone. I didn't ask anyone for help or support because it seemed ridiculous for a man to ask for help because his wife was abusing him.*
>
> —VINCENT

In addition, emotionally abusive women will use male stereotypes and gender roles against their partners. Alec, Pete, and Vincent describe ways they were abused by their female partners that other abused people will recognize, but they go on to share ways they were particularly susceptible to abuse as heterosexual men.

ALEC'S STORY

Like many other abusers, Alec's wife regularly showed disregard and disdain for him and sabotaged his efforts to spend time with his family and friends. In addition, she committed financial abuse by taking out credit cards and charging tens of thousands of dollars without his knowledge, and, ultimately, she had an affair. But she also used gender-related issues to manipulate him.

In traditional family arrangements where the man is the primary wage earner working outside the home and the woman is a homemaker and the primary caretaker for the children, a common complaint is that the man doesn't understand how hard it is to be a stay-at-home mom. Alec wanted to be supportive of his wife and took her complaints seriously. But in return, she took advantage of his good intentions:

> *I didn't know exactly how difficult it was to take care of a child. I didn't have any experience raising kids. I didn't have a baseline to compare it to. It wasn't until later that I could clearly see how other people do it. I started to see signs that she was not truthful. But for a long time, I believed her. I didn't know.*
>
> *She told me, "I take care of the kids all day—the hardest job in the world—so if you skip the gym today that would really help me." Her stuff always took priority. I adjusted all my social plans to accommodate hers. If I wanted to get a beer after work, I wouldn't go, or I'd skip going to the gym because she wanted to go do something. But that got to be almost every day. And what she was doing was she was having the social life she was manipulating me out of. That marriage taxed my social relationships to the point that they didn't exist anymore.*

(See more of Alec's story on page 109 where he describes how his wife didn't tend to meal preparation for the children or do their laundry, so he regularly had to take care of those things in addition to caring for the children when he got home from work.)

To be clear, being a stay-at-home parent is, indeed, a difficult and thankless job. Asking for and expecting help from the other partner is not wrong or abusive. What made this situation abusive was the deceit and manipulation that resulted in a gross imbalance in the family's division of labor as well as personal care and social time, benefiting one person at a high cost to the other.

Alec continues:

I also felt so belittled at times that I didn't want to bring those things up. She was always telling me about my inability to parent. I took a parenting class and someone in the class said, "Why are you even here?"

I was one of the younger people at work. I didn't have anyone in my age group to talk to, so I didn't know this wasn't normal.

I really wanted the marriage to work out, and at the time I didn't really think it was abnormal. So even though there were times when it didn't seem right, I didn't think it was that far out of the ordinary.

My advice? Fact check what you believe with friends, someone you don't mind opening up to who has no vested interest in your relationship other than an interest in you. Another key thing, the person who is being abused has to reach out to that other person, because it is very possible the other person sees it and doesn't want to approach you for fear of overstepping bounds.

Cut your losses. All their different methods rely on time. It takes time for their system to work. The longer you let it go on, the worse it is going to get.

PETE'S STORY

Pete experienced similar abuses as people in other abusive relationships: frequent and intense raging that led to isolation from his friends, family, and interests; extreme jealousy; and financial abuse. Beyond all those abuses, Pete's wife used gender issues against him when she threatened to harm herself and then accuse him of battering her:

> *She would threaten to stage an injury then tell the police I*
> *caused it. Once, we were in the car and she was angry at me.*
> *There was a policeman close by in a squad car. She said, "I'm*
> *going to have you arrested for hitting me." Then she banged*
> *her head against the car window to make a bruise.*

Pete also reported that his wife threatened to call the police and accuse him of sexually molesting her son because he wouldn't leave immediately to go get her a carton of cigarettes.

> *I always treated her rages and threats with de-escalation. I*
> *never was abusive. I used a calm, direct voice and asked her*
> *to be reasonable. I tried to defuse the conflict to protect the*
> *child in the household from witnessing violence.*
>
> *The thing I didn't do is abandon her or my stepson. I stayed*
> *because my stepson needed a stable person in his life, and I*
> *felt like I had a duty to care for my wife and provide for her*
> *irrespective of the abuse and the conflict.*

Pete took his role as a traditional family provider so seriously he stayed despite the abuse, yet his wife used that against him, too:

> *She would call me at work and berate me, saying I was incom-*
> *petent and if I worked more efficiently, I could be home sooner.*
> *She shamed me on my income and complained that I didn't*
> *make enough money.*
>
> *I probably should have left and gotten a divorce, but I acqui-*
> *esced for the benefit of the child.*

Pete's relationship with his wife ended when she died in her early forties. He continued to raise his stepson, and they went on to have a good relationship as adults.

VINCENT'S STORY

Like Pete, Vincent's wife frequently subjected him to aggressive anger by raging at him on a regular basis. But then she would turn the tables on him and accuse him of being an aggressive, toxic male.

> *If we were having a disagreement she would say, "Your pose is really aggressive. You're being very angry." So even though I was standing neutrally, I took what she said at face value, because that is a comment that is impossible to dispute. If she says, "Your body language is really aggressive," I can't tell her what she perceives, right?*

> *So, over the past four or five years when I'd see an argument coming, or if I was trying to convey a message that I knew was going to be difficult, or if the emotion in the room had just exploded, I would sit down in this yogi pose and say, "Ok, look this is not an aggressive pose. There is no way you can say this is aggressive." I tried to be as non-adversarial, non-aggressive, non-angry as possible.*

Women sometimes become submissive to minimize the threat of injury to themselves. In this case, the man took as nonthreatening a posture as possible to minimize the perception of a threat from him. One approach says, "Don't hurt me," the other says, "I have no intention of hurting you."

> *One night, she was shouting and screaming at me. I asked her to please stop. I asked for a moment of quiet, and she just kept screaming. I managed to lock myself in the guest bedroom and she stood outside the door, screaming, and shaking and hitting the door. This went on for almost four hours—shouting like that and hammering on the door.*

His wife swung from accusing him of being an aggressive male to making emasculating statements:

> *While out there, she was saying several variations of, "Open this door and face me like a man! I want a husband who has a penis!" I was not going to open the door because that situation was way too charged.*

While being emotionally and sometimes physically aggressive toward him, she took advantage of the male code of honor to never hit a woman:

> *I think the terrifying thing is she knows I'm never going to hit her. I'm never going to do anything violent or aggressive. I'm barely even going to protect myself against this because I don't want to cause more trouble. But it still hurts to hear those things from your partner who you want to protect and want to love physically and emotionally.*
>
> *One of my hobbies is obstacle racing, Spartan races. My other hobby is martial arts. I am very physically fit. If a person wants to, they could really hurt somebody with this stuff. To me the masculine ideal is someone who knows that and understands it and doesn't want that for anyone, doesn't want that situation. You step in, be calm, be steady, be of a reasonable mind, and you try make something better for somebody who needs it. I questioned myself for a long time. This is a new realization in the past few months that this is a perfectly good way to be a man. And in fact, this is better than a lot of other ways that society tells you to be a man.*

In addition to accusing Vincent of being aggressive, his wife would accuse him of saying things that were offensive when they were in social situations. She did that so often that he began to question his judgment and was reluctant to speak up, even at work. It wasn't until much later when other women gave him feedback that he realized that his wife had been gaslighting him.

After being interviewed for this book, Vincent wrote out a message to other heterosexual men being abused by their female partners:

> *First, in this specific dynamic—heterosexual woman abusing her husband—reverse the gender roles. Ask yourself, would this be appropriate for a man to do to a woman? Would I be okay with a man doing this to my daughter?*
>
> *Examples:*
>
> *We have slept in separate rooms for almost three years now, and the other night, she comes in, wakes me up, says she's sleeping in here tonight, and climbs into bed next to me. Chances are a hetero man wouldn't think twice about this— now reverse the gender roles, and a man crawls into bed next to a woman without asking her consent. This is super creepy. (See more of Vincent's experience with sexual abuse on page 176-177.)*
>
> *If a woman had shut herself in a guest bedroom for fear of being hit and her husband was on the other side of the door, shouting and pounding and demanding to be let in, that is terrifying. It's just as terrifying and wrong when it's a woman doing it to a man.*
>
> *Second, see a therapist. Interview three or more, just like you'd find someone to fix the roof, and see a good one. An excellent therapist will help you develop tools to confirm your experience, your reality, and help you start seeing what's really happening outside of someone else pounding a reality into you. This will be the first step in changing your life.*

Third, you aren't alone, and you aren't "less of a man." Society loves this explanation, and your abusive partner will utilize every tool she has available to tell you that what's going on is normal, acceptable, and above board, and make you question your own reality. This "less of a man" thing is a softball society just lets drift right over the plate for her to hit an easy home run. In fact, the opposite is probably true—people don't endure years of this if they aren't resilient and as tough as nails. You are way stronger than you think. But no one can endure it forever.

Finally, I'm answering these questions as specifically and accessibly as I can, because I read other people's experiences in other books and saw myself in them; they confirmed that I was experiencing abuse and that it was wrong. Reading that someone else was going through what I went through is what drove me over the starting line towards changing my life.

If any of this resonates, get responsible help and support. Get therapy. Whoever you are reading this, I believe in you.

NOTES

1. Bancroft, 2002, 2011; Engel, 1990, 2002; Evans, 1996; Lachkar 1998; Loring 1994.

2. Bancroft, 2002, 2011; Engel, 1990, 2002; Evans, 1996; Lachkar 1998; Loring 1994.

3. Loring, 1994.

4. Johnson, 2008; Loring, 1994; Pietromonaco & Collins, 2017.

5. Rogers, 1961.

6. Baumeister & Leary, 1995; Bowlby, 1988; Johnson, 2008; Pietromonaco & Collins, 2017; Ripoll-Núñez & Carrillo, 2016.

7. Baumeister & Leary, 1995; Coker, et. al., 2000; Johnson, 2008; Loring, 1994; Pietromonaco & Collins, 2017.

8. Dutton & Painter, 1993; Loring, 1994.

9. Bancroft, 2011; Dutton & Painter, 1993; Loring, 1994.

10. Baumeister & Leary, 1995; Johnson, 2008; Pietromonaco & Collins 2017.

11. Burkett & Young, 2012; Freeman 2017.

12. Loring, 1994.

13. Hollis, 1998.

14. Loring, 1994.

15. Johnson, 2008; Loring, 1994.

16. Baumeister & Leary, 1995; Johnson, 2008.

17. Bancroft, 2002; Evans, 1996; Herman, 1992.

18. Baumeister & Leary, 1995; Coker, et. al., 2000; Johnson, 2008; Loring, 1994; Pietromonaco & Collins, 2017.

19. Loring, 1994.

20. Pietromonaco & Collins 2017.

21. Coker, et. al., 2000.

22. Hazan and Shaver in Baumeister & Leary, 1995.

23. Johnson, 2008.

24. Coker, et. al.,2000; Johnson, 2008; Pietromonaco & Collins, 2017.

REFERENCES

Bancroft, L. (2002). *Why Does He Do That?* New York, NY: Berkley Books.

Bancroft, L. (2011). *Should I Stay or Should I Go?* New York, NY: Berkley Books.

Baumeister, R., & Leary, M. (1995). The Need to Belong: Desire for Interpersonal Attachments as a Fundamental Human Motivation. *Psychological Bulletin, 117*(3), 497-529. doi:10.1037/0033-2909.117.3.497.

Bowlby, J. (1988). *A Secure Base: Parent-Child Attachment and Healthy Human Development.* New York, NY: Basic Books.

Burkett, J., & Young, L. (2012). The Behavioral, Anatomical and Pharmacological Parallels Between Social Attachment, Love, and Addiction. *Psychopharmacology, 224* (1), 1-26. doi:10.1007/s00213-012-2794-x.

Chödrön, P. (2001). *The Places That Scare You: A Guide to Fearlessness in Difficult Times.* Boston, MA: Shambala Publications.

Dutton, D., & Painter, S. (1993). Emotional Attachments in Abusive Relationships: A Test of Traumatic Bonding Theory. *Violence and victims, 8*(2), 105-120.

Engel, B. (1990). *The Emotionally Abused Woman.* New York, NY: Fawcett Columbine.

Engel, B. (2002). *The Emotionally Abusive Relationship.* Hoboken, NJ: John Wiley and Sons.

Evans, P. (1993). *Verbal Abuse Survivors Speak Out on Relationship and Recovery.* Holbrook, MA: Bob Adams, Inc.

Evans, P. (1996). *The Verbally Abusive Relationship* (2nd ed.). Holbrook, MA: Adams Media Corporation.

Freeman PhD, R. (2017, January 18). The Brain Can Work Against Abuse Victims: The Hidden Ties to Toxic Partners. Retrieved from *Psychology Today*: https://www.psychologytoday.com/us/blog/neurosagacity/201701/the-brain-can-work-against-abuse-victims

Gottman, J. (1994). *Why Marriages Succeed or Fail: And How You Can Make Yours Last.* New York, NY: Fireside.

Gottman, J., Gottman, J. S., Abrams, D., & Abrams M.D., R. C. (2018). *Eight Dates: Essential Conversations for a Lifetime of Love.* New York, NY: Workman Publishing Co., Inc.

Herman, J. (1992). *Trauma and Recovery.* New York, NY: Basic Books.

Hollis, J. (1992). *The Eden Project: In Search of the Magical Other.* Toronto, ON: Inner City Books.

Johnson, S. (2008). *Hold Me Tight.* New York, NY: Brown Spark.

Lachkar, J. (1998). *The Many Faces of Abuse.* Northvale, NJ: Jason Aronson Inc.

Loring, M. (1994). *Emotional Abuse.* New York, NY: Lexington Books.

Pietromonaco, P., & Collins, N. (2017). Interpersonal Mechanisms Linking Close Relationships to Health. *The American Psychologist, 72*(6), 531-542. doi:10.1037/amp0000129.

Ripoll-Núñez, K., & Carrillo, S. (2016). Adult Intimate Relationships: Linkages Between Interpersonal Acceptance-Rejection Theory and Adult Attachment Theory. *Online Readings in Psychology and Culture, 6*(2). doi:10.9707/2307-0919.1149.

Rogers, C. (1961). *On Becoming a Person.* New York, NY: Houghton Mifflin Harcourt.

Walker, L. (1979). *The Battered Woman.* New York, NY: Harper & Row.

RECOMMENDED RESOURCES

The National Domestic Violence Hotline

The National Domestic Violence Hotline offers confidential support to people experiencing emotional abuse, as well as those facing physical abuse. Please contact them for assistance if you are confused about what is happening in your relationship, or if you feel your physical, mental, or emotional safety are or may be at risk.

To reach out for help in the USA, go to
www.thehotline.org/help

Or call: 1-800-799-7233.

The Hotline offers help in 140 different languages.

For resources in other countries check out:
en.wikipedia.org/wiki/List_of_domestic_violence_hotlines

How To Find A Co-Dependents Anonymous Meeting:
coda.org/find-a-meeting/

How To Find An Al-Anon Meeting:
al-anon.org/al-anon-meetings/find-an-al-anon-meeting/

How To Find An Adult Child Of Alcoholics Meeting:
adultchildren.org/meeting-search/

The phone numbers and email addresses above are accurate as of the time of publication. If you have trouble connecting with them, please research current information.

Additional Reading:

Bancroft, L. (2002). *Why Does He Do That?* New York, NY: Berkley Books.

Bancroft, L. (2011). *Should I Stay or Should I Go?* New York, NY: Berkley Books.

Beattie, M. (1992). *Codependent No More: How to Stop Controlling Others and Start Caring for Yourself.* Center City, MN: Hazelden Foundation.

Engel, B. (1990). *The Emotionally Abused Woman.* New York, NY: Fawcett Columbine.

Engel, B. (2021). *Escaping Emotional Abuse: Healing from the Shame You Don't Deserve.* New York, NY: Kensington Publishing Corp..

Evans, P. (1993). *Verbal Abuse Survivors Speak Out on Relationship and Recovery.* Holbrook, MA: Bob Adams, Inc.

Evans, P. (1996). *The Verbally Abusive Relationship* (2nd ed.). Holbrook, MA: Adams Media Corporation.

Lambert, C. (2016) *Women with Controlling Partners: Taking Back Your Life from a Manipulative or Abusive Partner.* Oakland, CA: New Harbringer Publications, Inc.

Mason, P., & Kreger, R. (2020). *Stop Walking on Eggshells: Taking Your Life Back When Someone You Care About Has Borderline Personality Disorder (3rd ed).* Oakland, CA: New Harbringer Publications, Inc.

Morningstar, D. (2017). *Start Here: A Crash Course in Understanding, Navigating, and Healing From Narcissistic Abuse.* Mason. MI: Morningstar Media

ABOUT THE AUTHOR

Mary Pat Haffey, MS, is a retired Licensed Professional Counselor. She worked with emotionally abused people during her internship and became interested in studying emotional abuse early in her career. She published an article, "Spiritual Principles and Partner Emotional Abuse" in the *Georgia Journal of Professional Counseling* in 2001. That article planted the seed that, after twenty years' experience, grew into this book, *Is It Supposed to Be This Hard? Telling the Difference Between Emotional Abuse and the Hard Work of Relationship.*